OUT OF THE DEPTHS

The Autobiography of John Newton

Introduction *by* HERBERT LOCKYER
Illustrations *by* RON McCARTY

Keats Publishing, Inc.   New Canaan, Connecticut

OUT OF THE DEPTHS
This autobiography was written in the form of letters to the Rev.
T. Haweis, D.D. and was first published in 1764.

Shepherd Illustrated Classic Edition published 1981
Special contents copyright © 1981 by Keats Publishing, Inc.

Library of Congress Catalog Card Number 80-85340
ISBN: 0-87983-243-6

Printed in the United States of America

SHEPHERD ILLUSTRATED CLASSICS are published by Keats
Publishing, Inc. 36 Grove Street, New Canaan, Connecticut 06840

He gives power to the faint & to him that
hath no might He increaseth strength.

CONTENTS

ILLUSTRATIONS

INTRODUCTION TO THE
SHEPHERD ILLUSTRATED CLASSICS EDITION

John Newton, the famed London preacher and hymn-writer who, in his *Olney Hymns*, taught the Church to sing his own devotional lyrics, *Amazing Grace* and *How Sweet the Name of Jesus Sounds*, wrote better than he knew, when over 200 years ago he gave the world his evangelical masterpiece—*Out of the Depths*. Truly, this remarkable Christian classic, in its new dress, has come to the kingdom for such a time as this. What an age of universal trouble and despair ours is! Scientists are telling us that a nuclear catastrophe is almost at the stroke of midnight. Well, we certainly need a spiritual magnet to draw us up out of our depths of sin, fear, depression and rumors of war; the reissue of Newton's soul-stirring volume provides such a magnet.

Perhaps a brief biographical sketch of this Anglican Church minister might help us to appreciate more fully the truths he set forth in this monumental and thrilling volume, proving the marvelous transforming power of God in a human life, which Newton originally penned in letter form. John Newton was born in London on July 24, 1725, and he came to occupy a unique position among Evangelicals of his time. Doubtless, the romance of his younger days, as well as the force of his character, made him the conspicuous power he became.

Newton's mother was a pious woman who filled his mind with Scripture, but she died when he was but seven years old. After two years of schooling, during which he learned the rudiments of Latin, he went to sea with his father. His life out on the deep sea was associated with vivid dreams, sailor recklessness and remarkable escapes from death. Gradually, he became an abandoned and godless sailor. His father had a heavy heart over the infidelity of his son, who at one time was flogged as a deserter from the British Navy and for over a year lived half-starved and ill-treated in abject degradation under an African slave-dealer. But God, who suddenly arrested another blasphemer, Saul of Tarsus, was about to display His amazing grace in the life of the sinful sailor.

One day John Newton read Thomas à Kempis's *Imitation of Christ*; this sowed the seed of his conversion, which he so vividly describes in his *Autobiography*, now in your hands. At twenty-three years of age, while steering a water-logged vessel in the face of apparent death, he came to realize his deep need of God. From 1748 through six years, he commanded a slave ship, and in a moment of revelation, turned to God, as he graphically recounts in *Out of the Depths*. Growing in grace, he forsook his sea-life, and for the next nine years he experienced rich and profitable fellowship with renowned revivalists like John Wesley and George Whitefield.

With a thirst for learning, Newton studied Hebrew and Greek and became a gifted author, giving to the world his *Olney Hymns*, *Omicron Letters*, and *Cardiphonia*, which Dr. Alexander Whyte kept on his "selectest shelf of spiritual books." Doubtless, it was his lifelong friendship with William Cowper, the renowned poet, that stimulated his own poetic gift.

It was in 1780 that Newton was appointed Rector of St. Mary Woolnoth Church in London, alongside the Bank of England in the heart of the metropolis, and for over twenty years this church was the center of a great widespread evangelical movement. His piety, zeal, warm heart and candor gained him the friendship of a reformer like William Wilberforce, who, through Newton's influence, came to abolish slavery. In 1805 John Newton's sight failed him and, being unable to read, he was pressed by his friends to retire, but his reply was: "What, shall the old African blasphemer stop when he can speak!"

Two years later, on December 20, 1807, John Newton went to be with the Lord whom he loved, and so devotedly served.

A few years ago I had the privilege of preaching from Newton's old pulpit at St. Mary Woolnoth in London, and after the service I stood beneath the plain marble tablet near the pulpit and read the epitaph which John Newton, himself, wrote and requested to be placed there after his death. It reads—

JOHN NEWTON, Clerk
Once an infidel and libertine
A servant of slaves in Africa,
Was, by the rich mercy of our Lord and Saviour
JESUS CHRIST,
restored, pardoned, and appointed to preach
the Gospel he had long laboured to destroy.
He ministered,
Near sixteen years at Olney, in Bucks,
And twenty-eight years in this Church.

Throughout Newton's experience at sea, the great restraining influence in his life was his deep love for Mary Catlett, whom he met when he was only seventeen and Mary but fourteen years old. So the conclusion of the above epitaph adds—

On February 1, 1750, he married
MARY
Daughter of the late George Catlett,
Of Chatham, Kent,
Whom he resigned to the Lord,

Who gave her,
On December 15, 1790.

Among Newton's well-known hymns is *Glorious Things of Thee are Spoken*, and in this, his *De Profundis*, he certainly magnifies the "glorious things" of God's saving grace and mercy. He tells us that he was religious in his own eyes, but often, instead of prayer, he learned to curse and blaspheme. But he came to confess, "Let me not fail to praise that grace which could expiate such sins as mine" . . . "The Lord beheld me with mercy. He did not strike me to Hell, as I justly deserved." . . . "I recollected the particulars of the life and death of Jesus for sins, not His own, but for those who in their distress would put their trust in Him" . . . "The goodness of the Father is receiving his prodigal son, nay, in running out to meet him, gained on me" . . . "The way of access to the throne of grace by the blood of Jesus was found, and peace was restored." . . . "It is sufficient that He knows how to dispose of me, and that He both can and will do what is best. To Him I commend myself. I trust that His will and my true interest are inseparable. To His name be glory."

If, after reading the full account of this soul-inspiring record of what God can do, yours is the Spirit-inspired desire to lead others out of the depth of their sin, why not give copies of this God-magnifying story of grace to your unsaved relatives and friends, praying that same will be used for their salvation. Who knows, you may win another John Newton for the Saviour!

Herbert Lockyer
February 1981

OUT OF
THE DEPTHS

Faith's Review and Expectation
I CHRONICLES 17:16–17

AMAZING grace! (how sweet the sound!)
    That saved a wretch like me;
I once was lost, but now am found;
    Was blind, but now I see.

'Twas grace that taught my heart to fear,
    And grace my fears relieved;
How precious did that grace appear
    The hour I first believed!

Through many dangers, toils, and snares,
    I have already come;
'Tis grace has brought me safe thus far,
    And grace will lead me home.

The Lord has promised good to me,
    His Word my hope secures;
He will my Shield and Portion be,
    As long as life endures.

Yes, when this flesh and heart shall fail,
    And mortal life shall cease,
I shall possess, within the vail,
    A life of joy and peace.

The earth shall soon dissolve like snow;
    The sun forbear to shine;
But God, who call'd me here below,
    Will be for ever mine.

LETTER I

REASONS FOR WRITING THE ACCOUNT

YOU HAVE AT TIMES had pleasing reflections on that promise to the Israelites, in Deuteronomy 8:2. They were then in the wilderness, surrounded with difficulties greatly aggravated by their distrust and perverseness. They had experienced a variety of dispensations, the design of which they could not as yet understand. They frequently lost sight of God's gracious purposes in their favor, and were much discouraged. Moses suggests to them that there was a future happy time drawing near when their journey and warfare should be finished. They should soon be put in possession of the promised land, and have rest from all their fears and troubles. Then it would give them pleasure to look back upon what they now found so uneasy to bear: "Thou shalt remember all the way which the Lord thy God led thee through the wilderness."

The importance and comfort of these words is still greater, if we consider them in a spiritual sense, as addressed to all who are passing through the wilderness of this world to a heavenly Canaan; who, by faith in the promises and power of God, are seeking an eternal rest in that kingdom which cannot be shaken. The hope of that glorious inheritance inspires us with some degree of

5

courage and zeal to press forward. When our eye is fixed upon the Lord, we are more than conquerors over all that would withstand our progress.

But we have not yet attained; we still feel the infirmities of a fallen nature. Through ignorance and unbelief, we often mistake the Lord's dealings with us, and are ready to complain. If we knew all, we should rejoice.

LOOKING BACK

But to us there is a time coming when our warfare shall be accomplished, our views enlarged, and our light increased. With what transports of adoration and love shall we look back upon the way by which the Lord led us! We shall then see and acknowledge that mercy and goodness directed every step; we shall see that what our ignorance once called adversities and evils, were in reality blessings which we could not have done well without. Nothing befell us without a cause; no trouble came upon us sooner or pressed on us more heavily, or continued longer than our case required. Our many afflictions were, each in their place, among the means employed by divine grace and wisdom to bring us to the possession of that exceeding and eternal weight of glory which the Lord has prepared for His people.

Even in this imperfect state, though we are seldom able to judge aright present circumstances, yet, if we look upon the years of our past, and compare what we have been brought through, with the frame of our minds under each successive period; if we consider how wonderfully one thing has been connected with another, so that what we now number among our greatest advantages, perhaps, took their first rise from incidents which we thought hardly worthy of our notice. We have sometimes escaped the greatest dangers that threatened, not by any wisdom or foresight of our own, but by the intervention of circumstances of which we neither desired nor thought. By the light offered us in the Scriptures, we may collect proof, from our narrow circle, that the wise and good providence of God watches over His people from the earliest moment of their lives, overrules and guards them through all their wanderings in a state of ignorance, and leads them in a way that they know not.

GOD'S WISE AND GOOD PROVIDENCE

I am persuaded, that every believer will see enough in his own case to confirm this; but not all in the same degree. The outward circumstances of many have been uniform—they have known but little variety in life; and with respect to their inward change, it has been effected in a secret way, unnoticed by others, and almost unperceived by themselves. The Lord has spoken to them, not in thunder and tempest; but with a still small voice He has drawn them gradually to Himself. Though they have a happy assurance that they know and love Him, and are passed from death unto life, yet of the precise time and manner they can give little account. Others He seems to select, in order to show the exceeding riches of His grace, and the greatness of His mighty power. He suffers the natural rebellion and wickedness of their hearts to have full scope; while other sinners are cut off with little warning, they are spared, though sinning with a high hand, and, as it were, studying their own destruction. At length, when all who know them are expecting to hear that they are made instances of divine vengeance, the Lord, whose thoughts are high above ours, as the heavens are higher than the earth, is pleased to pluck them as brands out of the fire—to make them monuments of His mercy, for the encouragement of others. They are, beyond expectation, convinced, pardoned, and changed.

A case of this indicates a divine power no less than the creation of a world: it is evidently the Lord's doing, and it is marvelous in the eyes of all those who are not blinded by prejudice and unbelief.

SAUL OF TARSUS

Persecuting Saul's heart was full of enmity against Jesus of Nazareth, therefore he persecuted and made havoc of His disciples.

He had been a terror to the church of Jersualem, and was going to Damascus with the same views. He was breathing out threatenings and slaughter against all that loved the Lord Jesus. He thought little of the mischief he had hitherto done. He was engaged for the suppression of the whole sect. Hurrying from house to house, from place to place, he carried menaces in his look, and repeated threatenings with every breath. The Lord Jesus, whom he hated and opposed, checked him in the height of his rage, called this bitter persecutor to the honor of an apostle, and inspired him to preach, with great zeal and earnestness, that faith which he so lately destroyed.

COLONEL GARDINER

Nor are we without remarkable displays of the same sovereign efficacious grace in our times. I particularly mention the instance of the late Colonel Gardiner. If any real satisfaction could be found in a sinful course, he would have met with it. He pursued the experiment with all possible advantages. He was habituated to evil; and many uncommon, almost miraculous, deliverances made no impression on him. Yet he was made willing in the day of God's power; and the bright example of his life, has afforded an occasion of much praise to God, and much comfort to His people.

After the mention of such, permit me to add my own name. These once eminent sinners proved eminent Christians: much had been forgiven them; they loved much. St. Paul could say, "The grace bestowed upon me was not in vain; for I labored more abundantly than they all." Colonel Gardiner was as a city set upon a hill, a burning and a shining light; the manner of his conversion was hardly more singular than the whole course of his conversation from that time to his death. It has not been that way with me. I must take deserved shame to myself. I have made very unsuitable returns for what I have received. If the question is only concerning the patience and longsuffering of God, the wonderful interposition of His providence in favor of an unworthy sinner, the power of His grace in softening the hardest heart, and the riches of His mercy in pardoning the enormous and aggravated transgressions, then in these respects I know no case more extraordinary than mine. Most, to whom I have related my story, have thought it worthy of being preserved.

THE FIRST LETTERS

I was deterred, on the one hand, by the great difficulty of writing properly when *self* is concerned; on the other, by the wrong use which persons of corrupt and perverse minds are often known to make of such instances. The psalmist reminds us that a reserve in these things is proper: "Come and hear, all ye that fear God, and I will declare what he hath done for my soul;" and our Lord cautions us not to "cast pearls before swine." The pearls of a Christian are, perhaps, his choice experiences of the Lord's power and love in the concerns of his soul.

These should not be at all adventures made public, lest we give occasion to earthly and groveling souls to profane what they cannot understand.

I yielded to the judgment and request of a much-respected friend, and sent him my story in a series of eight letters. I wrote to one person, but my letters have fallen into many hands. As you and other of my friends apprehend, my compliance with this request may be attended with some good effect, may promote the pleasing work of praise to our adorable Redeemer, or confirm the faith of some or other of His people, I am willing to obey. If God may be glorified on my behalf, and His children in any measure be comforted or instructed, by what I have to declare of His goodness, I shall be satisfied; I am content to leave all other possible consequences of this undertaking in His hands.

A MORE EXPLICIT NARRATIVE

I must again have recourse to memory, as I retained no copies of the letters. I hope you will excuse me if I do not strictly confine myself to narration, but now and then intersperse such reflections while I am writing.

I shall, therefore, if possible, write with that confidence and freedom which friendship and candor deserve.

LETTER II

YOUTHFUL DAYS

I CAN SOMETIMES FEEL pleasure in repeating the acknowledgment of David, "O Lord, I am Thy servant, the son of Thine handmaid; Thou hast loosed my bonds." The tender mercies of God toward me were manifested in the first moment of my life. I was born, as it were, in His house, and dedicated to Him in my infancy. My mother, as I have heard from many, was a pious, experienced Christian: she was a Dissenter, in communion with the late Dr. Jennings. I was her only child; she was of a weak constitution, and a retired temper. Almost her whole employment was the care of my education. I have some faint remembrance of her care and instructions. At not more than three years of age, she herself taught me English. When I was four years old I could read with propriety in any common book. She stored my memory, which was then very retentive, with many valuable pieces, chapters, and portions of Scripture, catechisms, hymns and poems.

ENCOURAGEMENT FOR PARENTS

At that time I had little inclination to the noisy sports of children, but was best pleased when in mother's company, and always as willing to learn as she was to teach. How far the best education may fall short of

11

reaching the heart will strongly appear in the sequel; yet I think, for the encouragement of godly parents to go on in the good way of doing their part faithfully, I may properly propose myself as an example. Though in process of time I sinned away all the advantages of these early impressions, yet they were for a great while a restraint upon me. They returned again and again, and it was very long before I could wholly shake them off. When the Lord at length opened my eyes, I found a great benefit from the recollection of them. My dear mother, besides the pains she took with me, often commended me with many prayers and tears to God.

My mother observed my early progress with peculiar pleasure, and intended from the first to bring me up with a view to the ministry, if the Lord should so incline my heart. In my sixth year I began to learn Latin. Before I had time to know much about it, the intended plan of my education was broken. The Lord's designs were far beyond the views of an earthly parent. He was pleased to reserve me for an unusual proof of His patience, providence, and grace; therefore overruled the purpose of my friends, by depriving me of my mother when I was under seven years old. I was born July 24, 1725, and she died July 11, 1732.

My father was at sea; he was a commander in the Mediterranean trade at that time. He came home the following year, and soon after married again, and I passed into different hands. I was well treated. The loss of my mother's instructions was not repaired. I was now permitted to mingle with careless profane children, and soon began to learn their ways. Soon after my father's marriage, I was sent to a boarding school in Essex, where the imprudent severity of the master almost broke my spirit and my relish for books. While with him I forgot the first principles and rules of arithmetic, which my mother had taught me years before. I stayed two years; in the last of the two, a new teacher came who observed and suited my temper, I took to Latin with great eagerness. Before I was ten years old, I read Tully and Virgil.

I believe I was pushed forward too fast. Not being grounded, I soon lost all I had learned (I left school in my tenth year). When I long afterward undertook Latin from books, I think I had little, if any advantage from what I had learned before.

EARLY SEA VOYAGES

When I was eleven years old my father took me to sea with him. A man of remarkable good sense, and great knowledge of the world, he took great care of my morals. But he could not supply my mother's part. Having been educated in Spain, he always observed an air of distance and severity in his carriage which overawed and discouraged my spirit. I was always in fear before him, and therefore he had the less influence.

From that time to the year 1742 I made several voyages, with considerable intervals between, chiefly in the country. A few months in my fifteenth year I was placed upon a very advantageous prospect at Alicant, Spain, but my unsettled behavior and impatience of restraint rendered that opportunity abortive.

In this period, my temper and conduct were exceedingly various. I had little concern about religion, and easily received very ill impressions. However I was often disturbed with convictions. I was fond of reading from a child. Among other books, Benet's "Christian

Oratory" came my way and though I understood but little of it, the course of life recommended appeared very desirable. I was inclined to attempt it; I began to pray, to read the Scriptures, and to keep a diary.

I was presently religious in my own eyes. But, alas! this seeming goodness had no solid foundation, but passed away like a morning-cloud, or the early dew. I was soon weary, gradually gave it up, and became worse than before. Instead of prayer, I learned to curse and blaspheme, and was exceedingly wicked when not under my parent's view.

Before I was twelve years old, I had a dangerous fall from a horse. Being thrown, unhurt, within a few inches of a hedgerow newly cut down, I could not avoid taking notice of a gracious Providence in my deliverance. Had I fallen upon the stakes I would inevitably have been killed. My conscience suggested to me the dreadful consequences if, in such a state, I had been summoned to appear before God.

I subsequently broke off my profane practices and appeared quite altered. But it was not long before I declined again. These struggles between sin and conscience were often repeated, and every relapse sank me into still greater depths of wickedness.

I was once roused by the loss of an intimate companion. We had agreed to go on board a man-of-war (I think it was on a Sunday); but I providentially came too late; the boat was overturned, and my friend and several others were drowned. I was invited to the funeral of my fellow, and was exceedingly affected to think that by a delay of a few minutes, which had much displeased and angered me, my life had been preserved. However, this likewise was soon forgotten.

"When I was eleven years old my father took me to sea with him."

At another time, the perusal of the "Family Instructor" put me upon a partial and transient reformation. In brief, though I cannot distinctly relate particulars, I think I took up and laid aside a religious profession three or four different times before I was sixteen years of age. All this while my heart was insincere.

I saw the necessity of religion as a means of escaping hell, but I loved sin, and was unwilling to forsake it. Instances of this I can remember, were frequent. In the middle of all my forms, I was strangely blind and stupid. Sometimes when determined upon things which I knew were sinful and contrary to my duty, I could not go on quietly till I had first dispatched my ordinary task of prayer. I grudged every moment of my time, but when this was finished, my conscience was in some measure pacified, and I could rush into folly with little remorse.

My last reform was the most remarkable, both for degree and continuance. Of this I may say in the apostle's words, "After the straitest sect of our religion I lived a Pharisee." I did everything that might be expected from a person entirely ignorant of God's righteousness, and desirous to establish his own. I spent the greatest part of every day in reading the Scriptures, meditation, and prayer. I fasted often; I even abstained from all animal food for three months; I would hardly answer a question for fear of speaking an idle word. I seemed to bemoan my former misconduct very earnestly, sometimes with tears.

I became an ascetic, and endeavored, so far as my situation would permit, to renounce society, that I might avoid temptation. I continued in this serious mood (I cannot give it a higher title) for more than two years without any considerable breaking off. It was poor religion. It left me, in many respects, under the power of sin. It tended to make me gloomy, stupid, unsociable, and useless.

Such was the frame of my mind when I became acquainted with Lord Shaftesbury's* *Characteristics.* The title allured me, and the style and manner gave me great pleasure, especially the second piece, which his lordship, with great propriety, entitled "A Rhapsody." Nothing could be more suited to my romantic mind than this pompous declamation. Of the design and tendency I was not aware; I thought the author a most religious person, and that I had only to follow him and be happy.

Thus, with fine words and fair speeches, my simple heart was beguiled. This book was always in my hand; I read it till I could very nearly repeat the "Rhapsody" *verbatim* from beginning to end. No immediate effect followed; but it operated like a slow poison, and prepared the way for all that came after.

In December, 1742, I returned from a voyage, and my father, not thinking of me for the sea again, was thinking how to settle me in the world. I had little life or spirit for business; I knew but little of men and things. I was fond of a visionary contemplative life, a medley of religion, philosophy, and indolence; and was quite averse to the thought of industrious application to business.

At length a merchant in Liverpool, an intimate friend of my father's (to whom, as the instrument of God's goodness, I have since been chiefly indebted for all my

---

*This was the third Lord Shaftesbury (1671–1713), whose writings excited great admiration in his day.

earthly comforts), proposed to send me for some years to Jamaica, and to charge himself with the care of my future. I consented to this, and was on the point of setting out the following week. In the meantime my father sent me on some business a few miles beyond Maidstone, in Kent. This little journey, which was to have been only for three or four days, occasioned a sudden and remarkable turn, which roused me from my indolence. "The way of man is not in himself; it is not in man that walketh to direct his steps."

LETTER III

EARLY LIFE AS A SAILOR

A FEW DAYS BEFORE my intended journey, I received an invitation to visit very intimate friends of my mother in Kent. Because of a coolness after my father's second marriage, I had heard nothing of them for many years.

I obtained my father's permission to call on them, but I was very indifferent about it and sometimes thought of passing on. However, I went. I was known at first sight, and met with the kindest reception, as the child of a dear, deceased friend.

My friends had two daughters. The eldest, as I learned some years after, had been considered by her mother and mine as a future wife for me, from the time of her birth. I do not say that my mother predicted what was to happen, yet there was something remarkable in the manner of its taking place.

All intercourse between the families had been long broken off; I was going into a foreign country and only called to pay a hasty visit. This I should not have thought of, but for a message received just at that crisis, for I had not been invited before. The circumstances were precarious in the highest degree, and the event extraordinary.

HIS FUTURE WIFE

Almost at the first sight of this girl (for she was then under fourteen) I felt an affection for her, which never abated or lost its influence a single moment in my heart. In degree, it equalled all that the writers of romance have imagined; in duration it was unalterable.

I soon lost all sense of religion, and became deaf to the remonstrances of conscience. But none of the misery I experienced ever banished her a single hour from my waking thoughts for seven years following.

Hardly anything less than this violent and commanding passion would have been sufficient to awaken me from the dull melancholy habit I had contracted. I was almost a misanthrope, notwithstanding I so much admired the pictures of virtue and benevolence as drawn by Lord Shaftesbury. Now my reluctance to active life was overcome, and I was willing to be or to do anything which might accomplish my wishes at some future time.

RESTRAINING EFFECT OF LOVE

When I later made shipwreck of faith, hope and conscience, my love to this person was the only remaining principle which in any degree took their place. The bare possibility of seeing her again was the only means of restraining me from the most horrid designs against myself and others.

But the ill effects it brought counterbalanced these advantages. Courtship is indeed a pleasing part of life, when there is a mutual affection, the consent of friends, a reasonable prospect as to settlement, and when it is conducted in subordination to the will and fear of God. But when these concomitants are wanting, what we call love is the most tormenting passion, and the most destructive in its consequences, that can be named.

And they were all wanting in my case. I dared not mention it to her friends or to my own, nor for a considerable time to her. I could make no proposals. It remained as a dark fire, locked up in my breast, which gave me constant uneasiness. It greatly weakened my sense of religion, and opened the way for the entrance of infidel principles. Though it seemed to promise great things, as an incentive to diligence and activity in life, in reality it performed nothing. I often considered what I would willingly do or suffer for the sake of her I loved; yet I was incapable of forcing myself away from her company to improve opportunities.

It did not prevent me from engaging in a long train of excess and riot, utterly unworthy of my honorable pretensions. And though, through the wonderful interposition of divine goodness, the maze of my follies was at length unraveled, I am sure I would not go through the same series of trouble again, to possess all the treasures of the Indies.

I now considered everything in a new light. I concluded it would be absolutely impossible to live at such a distance as Jamaica for a term of four or five years, and therefore determined that I would not go. I could not bear either to acquaint my father with the true reason or to invent a false one; therefore, without giving any notice to him why I did so, I stayed three weeks instead of three days in Kent. I thought the opportunity would be lost, and the ship would have sailed.

I then returned to London. I had highly displeased my father by this disobedience; but he was more easily reconciled than I expected. In a little time I sailed with a friend of his to Venice. In this voyage I was exposed to the company and bad example of the common sailors, among whom I ranked. Importunity and opportunity presenting every day, I once more began to relax from the sobriety and order which I had observed, in some degree, for more than two years.

I was sometimes pierced with sharp convictions. Though I made a few faint efforts to stop, I never recovered from this declension as I had from several before. I did not as yet turn out profligate, but I was making large strides toward total apostasy from God. The most remarkable warning I received (and the last) was a dream, which made a very strong, though not abiding impression on my mind.

HIS DREAM OF THE RING

The scene was the harbor of Venice, where we had lately been. I thought it was night, and my watch upon the dock. As I was walking to and fro by myself, someone brought me a ring, with an express charge to keep it carefully, assuring me that while I preserved that ring I should be happy and successful, but if I lost or parted with it, I must expect nothing but trouble and misery. I accepted the present and the terms willingly, not in the least doubting my own care to preserve it, and highly satisfied to have my happiness in my own keeping.

Then a second person came to me and, observing the ring on my finger, took occasion to ask some questions concerning it. I readily told him its virtues. He expressed surprise at my weakness in expecting such effects from a ring. He reasoned with me some time, and at length urged me to throw the ring away. At first I was shocked at the proposal, but his insinuations prevailed. I began to reason and doubt, and at last plucked it off my finger and dropped it over the ship's side into the water. At the same instant, a terrible fire burst out from a range of the mountains, a part of the Alps which appeared at some distance behind the city of Venice. I saw the hills as distinctly as if awake, and they were all in flames.

I perceived, too late, my folly. My tempter, with an air of insult, informed me that all the mercy of God in reserve for me was comprised in that ring, which I had wilfully thrown away. I understood that I must now go with him to the burning mountains, and that all the flames I saw were kindled on my account. I trembled, and was in a great agony, but my dream continued. As I stood self-condemned, without plea or hope, suddenly a third person, or the same who brought the ring at first (I am not certain which), came to me and demanded the cause of my grief. I told him plainly, confessing that I had ruined myself wilfully and deserved no pity. He blamed my rashness, and asked if I should be wiser supposing I had my ring again. I could hardly answer for I thought it was gone beyond recall. Indeed, I had not time to answer before I saw this unexpected friend go down under the water, just in the spot where I had dropped the ring. He soon returned, bringing it with him.

The moment he came on board, the flames in the mountains were extinguished, and my seducer left me. Then was "the prey taken from the hand of the mighty, and the lawful captive delivered." My fears were at an end, and with joy and gratitude I approached my kind deliverer to receive my ring again. But he refused to return it, and spoke to me: "If you should be entrusted with this ring again, you would very soon bring yourself into the same distress. You are not able to keep it, but I will preserve it for you. Whenever it is needful, I will produce it in your behalf."

I awoke in a state of mind not easy to be described. I could hardly eat or sleep, or transact my necessary business, for two or three days. But the impression soon wore off, and I totally forgot it. It hardly occurred to my mind again till several years afterward.

A time came when I found myself in circumstances very nearly resembling those suggested by this extraordinary dream, when I stood helpless and hopeless upon the brink of an awful eternity. Had the eyes of my mind been then opened, I should have seen my grand enemy, who had seduced me wilfully to renounce and cast away my religious professions, and to involve myself in complicated crimes. I should probably have seen him pleased with my agonies, and waiting for permission to seize and bear away my soul to his place of torment.

I should, perhaps, have seen likewise, that Jesus, whom I had persecuted and defied, rebuking the adversary, challenging me for His own, as a brand plucked out of the fire, and saying, "Deliver him from going down to the pit: I have found a ransom."

However, though I saw not these things, I found the benefit; I obtained mercy. The Lord answered for me in the day of my distress; and blessed be His name, He who restored the ring (or what was signified by it) vouchsafes to keep it. Oh, what an unspeakable comfort is this, that I am not in my own keeping! "The Lord is my Shepherd." I have been enabled to trust my all in

His Hands, and I know whom I have believed. Satan still desires to have me, that he might sift me as wheat, but my Saviour has prayed for me, that my faith may not fail. Here is my security and power, a bulwark against which the gates of Hell cannot prevail. But for this, many a time and often, if possible, I should have ruined myself since my first deliverance. Nay, I should fall and stumble and perish still, after all that the Lord has done for me, if His faithfulness were not engaged in my behalf, to be my Sun and Shield, even unto death. "Bless the Lord, O my soul."

Nothing very remarkable occurred in the following part of that voyage. I returned home in December, 1743, and soon after repeated my visit to Kent, where I protracted my stay in the same imprudent manner as before. This again disappointed my father and almost provoked him to disown me.

ON BOARD A MAN-OF-WAR

Before anything suitable offered again, I was pressured, owing entirely to my own thoughtless conduct, which was all of a piece, and put on board a tender: It was at a critical juncture, when the French fleets were hovering on our coast, so that my father was unable to procure my release. In a few days I was sent on board the *Harwich* at the Nore. I entered here upon quite a new scene of life, and endured much hardship for about a month.

My father was then willing that I should remain in the navy, as a war was daily expected, and procured a recommendation to the captain, who took me upon the quarter-deck as a midshipman. I had now an easy life as to externals, and might have gained respect, but my mind was unsettled; and my behavior very indifferent. I met with companions who completed the ruin of my principles. I affected to talk of virtue, and was not so outwardly abandoned as afterward, yet my delight and habitual practice was wickedness.

My chief intimate was a person of exceedingly good natural talents, and much observation. He was the greatest master of what is called the free-thinking scheme, and knew how to insinuate his sentiments in the most plausible way. He could hardly have labored more in the cause if he had expected to gain Heaven by it. This man, whom I honored as my master, and whose practice I adopted so eagerly, was overtaken in a voyage to Lisbon, by a violent storm. The vessel and people escaped, but a great sea broke on board, and swept him into eternity. Thus the Lord spares or punishes, according to His sovereign pleasure.

But to return: I was fond of his company. Having myself a smattering of books, I was eager enough to show my reading. He soon perceived that I had not wholly broken through the restraints of conscience, and therefore did not shock me at first with too broad intimations of his design. He rather spoke favorably of religion: but when he had gained my confidence, he began to speak plainer. Perceiving my ignorant attachment to the *Characteristics*, he joined issue with me on that book and convinced me that I never understood it.

He so plied me with objections and arguments that my depraved heart was soon gained, and I entered into his plan with all my spirit. Thus like an unwary sailor, who quits his port just before a rising storm, I renounced the hopes and comforts of the gospel, at the very time when every other comfort was about to fail me.

In December, 1744, the *Harwich* was in the Downs, bound for the East Indies. The captain gave me liberty to go on shore for a day. Imprudently disregarding consequences, I took horse, and followed the dictates of my restless passion to take a last leave of her I loved. I had little satisfaction in the interview, as I was sensible that I was taking pains to multiply my own troubles. The short time I could stay passed like a dream, and on New Year's day, 1745, I returned to the ship. The captain was prevailed on to excuse my absence. But this rash step, especially as it was not the first liberty I had taken, highly displeased him, and lost me his favor, which I never recovered.

At length we sailed from Spithead with a very large fleet. We put into Torbay with a change of wind, but turning fair again, we sailed the next day. Several of our fleet were lost in attempting to leave that place. The following night the whole fleet was greatly endangered on the coast of Cornwall by a storm from the southward. The darkness of the night, and the number of the vessels, occasioned much confusion and damage. Our ship, though several times in imminent danger of being run down by other vessels, escaped unhurt, but many suffered much, particularly the *Admiral*. This occasioned our putting back to Plymouth.

While we lay at Plymouth, I heard that my father, who had interest in some of the ships lately lost, had come down to Torbay. He had a connection at that time with the African Company. I thought, if I could get to him, he might easily introduce me into that service, which would be better than pursuing a long, uncertain voyage to the East Indies.

It was a maxim with me in those unhappy days, never to deliberate. The thought hardly occurred to me before I resolved to leave the ship at all events. I did so, and in the worst manner possible. I was sent one day in the boat, to take care that none of the people deserted. But I betrayed my trust, and went off myself. I knew not what road to take, and dared not ask for fear of being suspected. Having some general idea of the country, I guessed right, and when I had traveled some miles, I found upon inquiry, that I was on the road to Dartmouth.

All went smoothly that day, and part of the next. I had expected to be with my father in about two hours, when I was met by a small party of soldiers. I could not avoid or deceive them. They brought me back to Plymouth and walked through the streets guarded like a felon. My heart was full of indignation, shame and fear. I was confined two days in the guardhouse, then sent on board my ship, kept awhile in irons, then publicly stripped and whipped, after which I was degraded from my office. All my former companions were forbidden to show me the least favor, or even to speak to me. As a midshipman I had been entitled to some command, which, being haughty and vain, I had not been backward to exert. I was now brought down to a level with the lowest, and exposed to the insults of all.

My present situation was uncomfortable; my future prospects were still worse; the evils I suffered were likely to grow heavier every day. While my catastrophe was recent, the officers and my former shipmates were disposed to screen me from ill-usage; but during the little time I remained with them afterward, I found they cooled very fast in their endeavors to protect me. Indeed they could not avoid it without running a great risk of sharing with me. The captain, though in general a humane man who behaved very well to the ship's company, was almost implacable in his resentment when he had been greatly offended. He took several occasions to show himself so to me, and the voyage was to last for five years.

I think nothing I either felt or feared distressed me so much as to see myself thus forcibly torn away from the object of my affections under a great improbability of seeing her again, and a much greater of returning in such a manner as would give me hopes of seeing her mine. Thus I was as miserable on all hands as could well be imagined. My breast was filled with the most excruciating passions, eager desire, bitter rage, and black despair. Every hour exposed me to some new insult and hardship, with no hope of relief or mitigation, no friend to take my part or to listen to my complaint.

Inward or outward I could perceive nothing but darkness and misery. I think no case, except that of a conscience wounded by the wrath of God, could be more dreadful than mine. I cannot express with what wishfulness and regret I cast my last look upon the English shore. I kept my eyes fixed upon it till it disappeared. When I could see it no longer, I was tempted to throw myself into the sea. According to the wicked system I had adopted, this would put a period to all my sorrows at once. But the secret hand of God restrained me.

LETTER IV

VOYAGE TO AFRICA

THOUGH I DESIRED your instructions as to the manner and extent of these memoirs, I had already begun to write. When I began the eight letters, I intended to say no more of myself than might be necessary to illustrate the wonders of divine providence and grace in my life, but I account your judgment a sufficient warrant for enlarging my plan.

Among other things, you desired a more explicit account of my courtship. This was the point in which I thought it especially became me to be very brief, but I submit to you. This seems a proper place to tell you how it stood at the time of my leaving England.

When my inclinations were first discovered, both were so young, that no one but myself considered it in a serious view. It served for tea table talk among our friends, and nothing further was expected from it. But when my passion seemed to have abiding effects, so that in two years it was not at all abated, and especially as it occasioned me to act without any regard to prudence or interest, or my father's designs, and as there was a coolness between him and the family, her parents began to consider it as a matter of consequence. When I took my last leave of them, her mother, expressing the most tender affection for me, as if I had been her own child, told me, that she had no objections that at a maturer age there should be a probability of our engaging upon a prudent prospect. Yet as things then stood, she thought herself obliged to interfere. She therefore desired I would no more think of returning to their house, unless her daughter was away from home, till such time as I could either entirely give up my pretensions, or could assure her that I had my father's express consent to go on.

It was all difficult; but though she was young, gay, and quite unpracticed in such matters, she was directed to a happy medium. A positive encouragement, or an absolute refusal, would have been attended with equal, though different disadvantages. But without much study-ing about it, I found her always upon her guard. She had penetration to see her absolute power over me, and prudence to make a proper use of it. She would neither understand my hints, nor give me room to come to a direct explanation. She said since, that from the first discovery of my regard, and long before the thought was agreeable to her, she had often an unaccountable impression that sooner or later she should be mine. Upon these terms we parted.

NO FEAR OF GOD BEFORE HIS EYES

I return to my voyage. During our passage to Madeira, I was a prey to the most gloomy thoughts. Though I had well deserved all I met with, and the captain might have been justified if he had carried his resentment still further; yet my pride at that time suggested that I had been grossly injured. This so wrought upon my wicked heart, that I actually formed designs against his life; this was one reason that made me willing to prolong my own. I was sometimes divided between the two, not thinking it practicable to effect both.

The Lord had now to all appearances given me up to judicial hardness; I was capable of anything. I had not the least fear of God before my eyes, nor, so far as I remember, the least sensibility of conscience. I was possessed of so strong a spirit of delusion that I believed my own lie, and was firmly persuaded that after death I should cease to be. Yet the Lord preserved me! Some intervals of sober reflection would at times take place. When I had chosen death rather than life, a ray of hope would come in, though there was little probability for a hope, that I should yet see better days, and that I might again return to England and have my wishes crowned, if I did not wilfully throw myself away.

My love was now the only restraint I had left. Though I neither feared God nor regarded men, I could not bear that she should think meanly of me when I was dead. As in the outward concerns of life the weakest means are often employed by divine providence to produce great effects beyond their common influence, for instance, a disease removed by a fright, so I found it then. This single thought, which had not restrained me from a thousand smaller evils, proved my only and effectual barrier against the greatest and most fatal temptations. How long I could have supported this conflict, or what, humanly speaking, would have been the consequences of my continuing in that situation, I cannot say. The Lord, whom I little thought of, knew my danger, and was providing for my deliverance.

DISCHARGED FROM H.M.S. HARWICH

Two things I had determined when at Plymouth: that I would not go to India, and that I would go to Guinea. Such indeed was the Lord's will concerning me; but they were to be accomplished in His way, not in mine.

We had been at Madeira some time. The business of the fleet was completed, and we were to sail the following day. On that memorable morning I was late in bed. I would have slept longer, but one of the midshipmen, an old companion, came down, and between jest and earnest bade me rise. As I did not immediately comply he cut down the hammock in which I lay, which forced me to dress myself. I was very angry, but dared not resent it. I was little aware how much his caprice affected me! This person, who had no design in what he did, was the messenger of God's providence. I said little, but went upon deck, where I that moment saw a man putting his clothes into a boat, who told me he was going to leave us. Upon inquiring, I was informed that two men, from a Guinea ship, which lay near us, had entered on board the *Harwich*, and that the commodore, Sir George Pocock, had ordered the captain to send two others in their room.

My heart instantly burned like fire. I begged the boat might be detained a few minutes: I ran to the lieutenant, and entreated him to intercede with the captain that I might be dismissed. Though I had been formerly upon ill terms with these officers, and had disobliged them all in their turns, yet they had pitied my case, and were ready to serve me now. The captain, who, when we were at Plymouth, had refused to exchange me at the request of Admiral Medley, was now easily pre-

"As I did not immediately comply he cut down the hammock in which I lay . . ."

vailed on. In little more than half an hour from my being asleep in bed I saw myself discharged, and safe on board another ship.

This was one of the many critical turns of my life in which the Lord was pleased to display His providence and care by causing many unexpected circumstances to concur in almost an instant of time. These sudden opportunities were several times repeated; each of them brought me into an entirely new scene of action, and they were usually delayed to almost the last moment in which they could have taken place.

SINNING WITH A HIGH HAND

The ship I went on board was bound for Sierra Leone, and the adjacent parts of what is called the Windward Coast of Africa. The commander, I found, was acquainted with my father. He received me very kindly and made fair professions of assistance. I believe he would have been my friend, but without making the least advantage of former mistakes and troubles, I pursued the same course. If possible I acted much worse.

On board the *Harwich*, though my principles were totally corrupted, at first I was in some degree staid and serious. The remembrance of this made me ashamed of breaking out in that notorious manner I could otherwise have indulged. But now, entering among strangers, I could appear without disguise. I well remember that while I was passing from the one ship to the other, this was one reason why I rejoiced in the exchange. One reflection I made upon the occasion was "that I now might be as abandoned as I pleased, without any control." From this time I was exceedingly vile indeed, little if anything short of that animated description of an almost irrecoverable state which we have in II Peter 2:14.

I not only sinned with a high hand myself, but made it my study to tempt and seduce others upon every occasion. I eagerly sought occasion, sometimes to my own hazard and hurt. One natural consequence of this was a loss of favor with my new captain. Not that he was at all religious, or disliked my wickedness more than it affected his interest, but I became careless and disobedient. I did not please him because I did not intend it, and as he was a man of an odd temper likewise we the more easily disagreed. Besides, I had a little of that unlucky wit which can multiply troubles and enemies to its possessor. Upon some imagined affront, I made a song, in which I ridiculed his ship, his designs, and his person, and soon taught it to the whole ship's company. Such was the ungrateful return I made for his offers of friendship and protection. I had mentioned no names, but the allusion was plain and he was no stranger either to the intention or the author. I shall say no more of this part of my story; let it be buried in eternal silence.

But let me not fail to praise that grace which could pardon, that blood which could expiate, such sins as mine. Yea, "the Ethiopian may change his skin, and the leopard his spots." I, who was the willing slave of every evil, possessed with a legion of unclean spirits, have been spared and saved, and changed, to stand as a monument of His almighty power for ever.

Thus I went on for about six months, by which time the ship was preparing to leave the coast. A few days before she sailed the captain died. I was not upon much better terms with his mate who now succeeded to the command, and had upon some occasion treated me ill. I had no doubt that if I went with him to the West Indies, he would put me on board a man-of-war, and this, from what I had known already, was more dreadful to me than death. To avoid it, I determined to remain in Africa, and amused myself with many golden dreams that here I should find an opportunity of improving my fortune.

ENTERS THE SLAVE TRADE

There are still upon that part of the coast a few white men settled. There were many more at the time I was first there, whose business it was to purchase slaves in the rivers and country adjacent, and sell them to the ships at an advanced price.

One of these who at first landed in my indigent circumstances had acquired considerable wealth. He had lately been in England, and was returning to the vessel I was in, of which he owned a quarter part. His example impressed me with the hopes of the same success, and upon condition of entering into his service, I obtained my discharge. I had not the precaution to make my terms, but trusted to his generosity. I received no compensation for my time on board the ship, but a bill upon the owners in England. This was never paid, for they failed before my return. The day the vessel sailed, I landed upon the island of Benanoes, with little more than the clothes upon my back, as if I had escaped shipwreck.

LETTER V

TRIALS IN WEST AFRICA

THERE SEEMS an important instruction in these words of our dear Lord, "Mine hour is not yet come." The two following years, of which I am now to give some account, will seem as an absolute blank in a very short life: but as the Lord's hour of grace was not yet come, I was to have still deeper experience of the dreadful state of the heart of man when left to itself. I have seen frequent cause since to admire the mercy of the Lord in banishing me to those distant parts, and almost excluding me from human society, at a time when I was big with mischief, and, like one infected with a pestilence, was capable of spreading a taint wherever I went.

Had my affairs taken a different turn; had I succeeded in my designs, and remained in England, my sad story would probably have been worse. Worse in myself indeed, I could hardly have been, but my wickedness would have had greater scope: I might have been very hurtful to others, and multiplied irreparable evils. But the Lord wisely placed me where I could do others little harm. The few I had to converse with were too much like myself, and I was soon brought into such abject circumstances that I was too low to have any influence. I was rather shunned and despised than imi-

36

tated, there being few, even of the negroes themselves, during the first year of my residence among them, but thought themselves too good to speak to me.

I was as yet an "outcast lying in my blood" (Ezek. 16:6); and to all appearance, exposed to perish. But the Lord beheld me with mercy. He did not strike me to Hell, as I justly deserved; "He passed by me when I was in my blood, and said unto me, Live." The appointed time for the manifestation of His love to cover all my iniquities with the robe of His righteousness, and to admit me to the privileges of His children, was not till long afterward; yet He bade me live. I can only ascribe it to His secret upholding power, that what I suffered in a part of this interval did not bereave me either of my life or senses; yet, since by these sufferings the force of my evil example and inclination was lessened, I have reason to account them amongst my mercies.

It may not be amiss to give you a very brief sketch of the geography of the circuit I was now confined to. I may have frequent occasion to refer to places that I shall now mention, for my trade afterward, when the Lord gave me to see better days, was chiefly to the same places, and with the same persons, where and by whom I had been considered on a level with their meanest slaves.

From Cape de Verd, the most western point of Africa, to Cape Mount, the whole coast is full of rivers; the principal are, Gambia, Rio Grande, Sierra Leone, and Sherbro. Of the former, as it is well known, and as I was never there, I need say nothing. The Rio Grande, like the Nile, divides into many branches near the sea. On the most northerly, called Cacheo, the Portuguese have a settlement. The most southern branch, known by the name of Rio Nuna, is, or then was, the usual boundary of the white men's trade northward. Sierra Leone is a mountainous peninsula, uninhabited, and inaccessible on account of the thick woods, excepting those parts which lie near the water.

The river is large and navigable. About twelve leagues to the southeast, are three contiguous islands, called the Benanoes, about twenty miles in circuit. This was about the center of the white men's residence.

Seven leagues farther, the same way, lie the Plantanes, three small islands, two miles distant from the continent at the point which forms one side of the Sherbro. This river is more properly a sound running within a long island, and receiving the confluences of several large rivers, "rivers unknown to song," but far more deeply engraven in my remembrance than the Po or Tiber. The southernmost of these has a very peculiar course, almost parallel to the coast. It will seldom lead one above three miles, and sometimes not more than half a mile from the seashore. Indeed, I know not but that all these rivers may have communications with each other, and with the sea in many places. If you cast your eyes upon a large map of Africa, you will have a general idea of the country I was in. Most of the places I have mentioned are in the same order as I have named them.*

My new master had formerly resided near Cape Mount, but now he settled at the Plantanes, upon the largest of the three islands. It is a low sandy island, about two miles in circumference, and almost covered with palm

---

*The geographical description is inserted as Newton wrote it, but the reader will bear in mind the changes that have occurred during a long interval of time.

trees. We immediately began to build a house, and to enter upon trade. I had now some desire to retrieve my lost time, and to exert diligence in what was before me. He was a man with whom I might have lived tolerably well, if he had not been soon influenced against me. He was much under the direction of a black woman, who lived with him as a wife. She was a person of some consequence in her own country, and he owed his first rise to her interest. The woman, I know not for what reason, was strangely prejudiced against me from the first. What made it still worse for me was a severe illness which attacked me very soon, before I had opportunity to show what I could or would do in his service.

TREATED WITH SCORN AND CONTEMPT

I was sick when he sailed in a shallop to Rio Nuna, and he left me in the woman's hands. At first I was taken some care of, but as I did not recover very soon, she grew weary and entirely neglected me. I had sometimes not a little difficulty to procure a draught of cold water when burning with a fever. My bed was a mat spread upon a board or chest, and a log of wood my pillow. When my fever left me, and my appetite returned, I would gladly have eaten, but no one gave me. She lived in plenty herself, but hardly allowed me sufficient to sustain life. Now and then, when in the highest good humor, she would send me victuals in her own plate after she had dined. So greatly was my pride humbled, I received this with thanks and eagerness, as the most needy beggar does an alms.

Once, I well remember, I was called to receive this bounty from her own hand, but being exceedingly weak and feeble, I dropped the plate. Those who live in plenty can hardly conceive how this loss touched me, but she had the cruelty to laugh at my disappointment. Though the table was covered with dishes (she lived much in the European manner) she refused to give me any more. My distress has been at times so great as to compel me to go by night and pull up roots in the plantation at the risk of being punished as a thief. These I have eaten raw upon the spot, for fear of discovery. The roots I speak of are very wholesome food, when boiled or roasted, but as unfit to be eaten raw in any quantity as a potato.

I have sometimes been relieved by strangers, even by slaves in the chain, who have secretly brought me victuals (for they dared not be seen) from their own slender pittance.

Next to pressing want, nothing sits harder upon the mind than scorn and contempt. Of this I had an abundant measure. When I was very slowly recovering this woman would sometimes pay me a visit, not to pity or relieve, but to insult me. She would call me worthless and indolent, and compel me to walk, which I could hardly do. She would then send her attendants to mimic my motion, to clap their hands, laugh and throw limes at me. If they chose to throw stones, as was the case once or twice, they were not rebuked. Though all who depended on her favor must join in her treatment, yet, when she was out of sight, I was rather pitied than scorned by the meanest of her slaves.

ACCUSED WITH DISHONESTY

At length my master returned from his voyage. I complained of ill-usage, but he could not believe me;

and as I did it in her hearing, I fared no better for it. But in his second voyage he took me with him. We did pretty well for a while, till a brother trader he met in the river persuaded him that I was unfaithful, that I stole his goods in the night or when he was on shore. This was almost the only vice I could not be justly charged with. The only remains of a good education I could boast of was what is commonly called honesty. As far as he had entrusted me, I had been always faithful. Though my great distress might, in some measure, have excused it, I never once thought of defrauding him in the smallest matter. However, the charge was believed, and I was condemned without evidence.

HUNGER AND EXPOSURE

From that time he likewise used me very hardly. Whenever he left the vessel, I was locked upon deck, with a pint of rice for my day's allowance, and if he stayed longer, I had no relief till his return. Indeed, I believe I should have been nearly starved but for an opportunity of catching fish sometimes. When fowls were killed for his own use, I seldom was allowed any part but the entrails to bait my hooks with. At what we call slack water, that is, about the changing of the tides, when the current was still, I used generally to fish, for at other times it was not practicable; and I very often succeeded. If I saw a fish upon my hook my joy was little less than any other person may have found in the accomplishment of the scheme he had most at heart. Such a fish, hastily broiled, or rather, half burned, without sauce, salt, or bread, has afforded me a delicious meal.

If I caught none, I might, if I could, sleep away my

hunger till the return of slack water, and then try again. Nor did I suffer less from the inclemency of the weather, and the want of clothes. The rainy season was now advancing. My clothing was a shirt, a pair of trousers, a cotton handkerchief, instead of a cap, and a cotton cloth, about two yards long for upper garments. Thus accoutred, I have been exposed for twenty, thirty, perhaps nearly forty hours together, in incessant rains, accompanied with strong gales of wind, without the least shelter, when my master was on shore.

I feel some faint returns of the violent pains I then contracted. The excessive cold and wet I endured in that voyage, and so soon after I had recovered from a long sickness, quite broke my constitution and my spirits. The latter were soon restored; but the effects of the former still remain with me as a needful memento of the service and wages of sin.

In about two months we returned. The rest of the time I remained with him was chiefly spent at the Platanes, under the same regimen as I have already mentioned. My haughty heart was now brought down, not to a wholesome repentance, nor to the language of the prodigal— this was far from me—but my spirits were sunk, and I lost all resolution, and almost all reflection. I had lost the fierceness which fired me on board the *Harwich*, and which made me capable of the most desperate attempts. But I was no further changed than a tiger tamed by hunger. Remove the occasion, and he will be as wild as ever.

One thing, though strange, is true. Though destitute of food and clothing, depressed to a degree beyond common wretchedness, I could sometimes collect my mind to mathematical studies. I had bought Barrow's

Euclid at Plymouth. It was the only volume I brought on shore. It was always with me, and I used to take it to remote corners of the island by the seaside and draw my diagrams with a long stick upon the sand. Thus I often beguiled my sorrows, and almost forgot my feeling. Without any other assistance, I made myself, in a good measure, master of the first six books of *Euclid*.

LETTER VI

ENTERS THE SERVICE OF A NEW MASTER

THERE IS MUCH PIETY and spirit in the grateful acknowledgment of Jacob, "With my staff I passed over this Jordan, and now I am become two bands." These are words which ought to affect me with a peculiar emotion. I remember that some of those mournful days to which my last letter refers, I was busied in planting some lime or lemon trees. The plants I put in the ground were no longer than a young gooseberry-bush. My master and his mistress, passing by the place, stopped awhile to look at me. "Who knows," said he, "who knows but by the time these trees grow up and bear, you may go home to England, obtain the command of a ship, and return to reap the fruits of your labors? We see strange things sometimes happen." This, as he intended it, was a cutting sarcasm. I believe he thought it as probable that I should live to be king of Poland. Yet it proved a prediction, and one of them at least lived to see me return from England in the capacity he had mentioned, and pluck some of the first limes from those very trees. How can I proceed till I raise a monument to the divine goodness, by comparing the circumstances in which the Lord has since placed me, with what I was at that time!

44

Had you seen me go, pensive and solitary, in the dead of night to wash my one shirt upon the rocks, and afterward put it on wet, that it might dry upon my back while I slept; had you seen me so poor a figure, that when a ship's boat came to the island shame often constrained me to hide myself in the woods from the sight of strangers; especially had you known that my conduct, principles, and heart, were still darker than my outward condition—how little would you have imagined, that one who so fully answered to the description of the apostle— "hateful and hating one another"—was reserved to be so peculiar an instance of the providential care and exuberant goodness of God!

There was, at that time, but one earnest desire in my heart which was not contrary and shocking both to religion and reason. That one desire, though my vile, licentious life rendered me peculiarly unworthy of success, and though a thousand difficulties seemed to render it impossible, the Lord was pleased to gratify. But this favor though great, and greatly prized, was a small thing, compared to the blessings of His grace. He spared me to give me "the knowledge of himself, in the person of Jesus Christ." In love to my soul, He delivered me from the pity of corruption, and cast all my aggravated sins behind His back. He brought my feet into the paths of peace.

When He made me acceptable to Himself in the Beloved, He gave me favor in the sight of others. He raised me new friends, protected and guided me through a long series of dangers, and crowned every day with repeated mercies. To Him I owe it that I am still alive, and that I am not still living in hunger, in thirst, in nakedness, and the want of all things. Into that state I brought myself, but it was He who delivered me. He has given me an easy situation in life, some experimental knowledge of His gospel, a large acquaintance among His people, a friendship and correspondence with several of His most honored servants. It is as difficult to enumerate my present advantages as it is fully to describe the evils and miseries of the preceding contrast.

I know not exactly how long things continued thus with me, but I believe nearly a year. In this interval I wrote two or three times to my father. I gave him an account of my condition, and desired his assistance, intimating at the same time that I had resolved not to return to England unless he was pleased to send for me. I have likewise letters written to the one I loved in that dismal period. At the lowest ebb, it seems, I still retained a hope of seeing her again. My father applied to his friend in Liverpool, of whom I have spoken before. He gave orders, accordingly, to a captain of his own who was then fitting out for Gambia and Sierra Leone.

BETTER CIRCUMSTANCES

Within the year, as I have said, I obtained my master's consent to live with another trader on the same island. Without his consent I could not be taken. He was unwilling to do it sooner, but it was then brought about. This was much to my advantage: I was soon decently clothed, lived in plenty, was considered as a companion, and trusted with the care of all his domestic effects, to the amount in money of some thousand pounds.

This man had several factories and white servants in different places particularly one in Kittam, the river which runs so nearly along the seacoast. I was soon appointed to go there, where I had a share in the management of business, jointly with another of his servants. We lived as we pleased, business flourished, and our employer was satisfied.

I began to be wretch enough to think myself happy. There is a significant phrase frequently used in those parts that such a white man has grown *black*. It does not intend an alteration of complexion, but disposition. I have known several, who, settling in Africa after the age of thirty or forty, have at that time of life been gradually assimilated to the tempers, customs, and ceremonies of the natives, so far as to prefer that country to their own. They have even become dupes to all the pretended charms, necromancies, amulets, and divinations of the blinded negroes, and put more trust in such things than the wiser sort among the natives. A part of this spirit of infatuation was growing upon me. In time, perhaps, I might have yielded to the whole. I entered into closer engagements with the inhabitants, and should have lived and died a wretch among them, if the Lord had not watched over me for good. Not that I had lost those ideas which chiefly engaged my heart to England, but despair of seeing them accomplished made me willing to remain where I was. I thought I could more easily bear the disappointment in this situation than nearer home.

But as soon as I had fixed my connections and plans with these views, the Lord providentially interposed to break them in pieces, and to save me from ruin in spite of myself.

In the meantime the ship that had orders to bring me home arrived at Sierra Leone. The captain made inquiry for me there, and at the Benanoes; but understanding that I was at a great distance in the country, he thought no more about me. Without doubt the hand of God directed my being placed at Kittam just at this time. As the ship came no nearer than the Benanoes, and stayed but a few days, if I had been at the Plantanes I should not perhaps have heard of her till she had sailed. The same must have certainly been the event had I been sent to any other factory of which my new master had several. But though this place was more than a hundred miles' distance from the Plantanes, yet I was still within a mile of the seacoast.

More remarkable, I was at that very juncture going in quest of trade, to a place some distance from the sea. I should have set out a day or two before, but we had waited for a few articles from the next ship to complete the assortment of goods I was to take with me. We used sometimes to walk on the beach, in expectation of seeing a vessel pass by, but this was very precarious, as at this time the place was not resorted to by ships for trade. I do not know that any had stopped while I was there, though some had before, upon observing a signal made from the shore.

FREED FROM A CAPTIVITY OF
FIFTEEN MONTHS

In February, 1747, I know not the exact day, my fellow-servant, walking down to the beach in the afternoon, saw a vessel sailing past, and made a smoke in token of trade. She was already a little beyond the place, and as the wind was fair, the captain was in doubt whether to stop or not. However, half an hour later, the ship would have gone beyond recall. When my companion saw her come to an anchor, he went on board from a canoe. One of the first questions he was asked was concerning me. When the captain understood I was so near, he came on shore to deliver his message. Had an invitation from home reached me when I was sick and starving at the Plantanes, I should have received it as life from the dead, but now, for the reasons already given, I heard it at first with indifference. The captain, unwilling to lose me, told a story altogether of his own framing. He gave me a very plausible account how he had missed a large packet of letters and papers which he should have brought with him. But this he said he was sure of—having had it from my father's own mouth, as well as from his employer—that a person lately dead had left me four hundred a year; adding further, that if I was any way embarrassed in my circumstances, he had express orders to redeem me, though it should cost one half of his cargo. Every particular of this was false. I could hardly believe what he said about the estate, but as I had some expectation from an aged relative I thought a part of it might be true.

I was not long in suspense. Though my father's care and desire to see me had too little weight with me, and would have been insufficient to make me quit my retreat, the remembrance of my loved one, the hope of seeing her, and the possibility that accepting this offer might once more put me in a way of gaining her hand, prevailed over all other considerations.

The captain further promised (and in this he kept his word) that I should lodge in his cabin, dine at his table, and be his constant companion, without his expecting any service from me. Thus I was suddenly freed from a captivity of about fifteen months. I had neither a thought nor a desire of this change one hour before it took place. I embarked with him, and in a few hours lost sight of Kittam.

GOD'S RULING POWER AND WISDOM

So blind and stupid was I at that time, I made no reflection, I sought no direction in what had happened. Like a wave of the sea driven with the wind, and tossed, I was governed by present appearances, and looked no further. But He who is eyes to the blind, was leading me in a way that I knew not.

Now I am in some measure enlightened, I can easily perceive that it is in these seemingly fortuitous circumstances, that the ruling power and wisdom of God are most evidently displayed in human affairs. How many such casual events in the history of Joseph, had each a necessary influence on his ensuing promotion! If he had not dreamed, or if he had not told his dream; if the Midianites had passed by a day sooner, or a day later; if they had sold him to any person but Potiphar; if his mistress had been a better woman; if Pharaoh's officers had not displeased their lord; or if any or all these things had fallen out in any other manner or time than they did, all that followed would have been different. The promises and purposes of God concerning Israel, their bondage, deliverance, polity, and settlement, must have failed. If history had not been as it was according to God's plan, then the promised Saviour, the Desire of all nations, would not have appeared. Mankind had been still in their sins, without hope, and the counsels of God's eternal love in favor of sinners defeated.

Thus we may see a connection between Joseph's first

dream and the death of our Lord Christ, with all its glorious consequences, so strong, though secret, is the concatenation between the greatest and the smallest events. What a comfortable thought is this to be a believer, to know that amid all the various interfering designs of men, the Lord has one constant design, which He cannot, will not miss, namely, His own glory in the complete salvation of His people; and that He is wise, and strong, and faithful, to make even those things which seem contrary to this design, subservient to promote it.

LETTER VII

DANGERS AND DELIVERANCES

THE SHIP I WAS NOW ON as a passenger was on a trading voyage for gold, ivory, dyers' wood and beeswax. It requires much longer time to collect a cargo of this sort than of slaves. The captain had begun his trade at Gambia, had been already four or five months in Africa, and continued about a year after I was with him. We ranged the whole coast as far as Cape Lopez, which lies about a degree south of the equinoctial, and more than a thousand miles farther from England than the place where I embarked.

I had no business to employ my thoughts, but sometimes amused myself with mathematics. Excepting this, my life, when awake, was a course of most horrid impiety and profaneness I know not that I have ever since met so daring a blasphemer. Not content with common oaths and imprecations, I daily invented new ones, so that I was often seriously reproved by the captain, who was a very passionate man and not at all circumspect in his expressions.

A JONAH ON BOARD

From what I told him of my past adventures and what he saw of my conduct, especially toward the close of the voyage, when he met with many disasters. He would often tell me that to his grief he had a Jonah on board; that a curse attended me wherever I went, and that all the troubles he met with in the voyage were owing to his having taken me into the vessel.

Although I lived long in the excess of almost every other extravagance, I never was fond of drinking. My father has often been heard to say that while I avoided drunkenness, he should still entertain hopes of my recovery. But sometimes I would promote a drinking bout for the sake of a frolic, as I called it. Although I did not love the liquor, I was sold to do iniquity, and delighted in mischief.

The last abominable frolic of this sort I engaged in was in the river Gabon; the proposal and expense were my own. Four or five of us one evening sat down upon deck to see who could hold out longest in drinking geneva and rum alternately. A large sea shell supplied the place of a glass. I was very unfit for a challenge of this sort, for my head was always incapable of bearing much strong drink. However, I proposed the first toast, which I well remember was some imprecation against the person who should *start* first. This proved to be myself.

AN AMAZING ESCAPE

My brain was soon fired, I arose and danced about the deck like a madman. While I was thus diverting my companions, my hat went overboard. By the light of the moon I saw the ship's boat, and eagerly threw myself over the side to get into her, that I might recover my hat. The boat was not within my reach as I thought, but perhaps twenty feet from the ship's side. I was half

over, and should in one moment more have plunged
into the water when somebody caught hold of my clothes
behind and pulled me back. This was an amazing escape. I could not swim, if I had been sober; the tide ran
very strong; my companions were too intoxicated to
save me; and the rest of the ship's company were asleep.
So near was I to perishing in that dreadful condition,
and sinking into eternity under the weight of my own
curse!

Another time, at Cape Lopez, some of us had been in
the woods, and shot a buffalo or wild cow. We brought
a part of it on board, and carefully marked the place, as
I thought, where we left the remainder. In the evening
we returned to fetch it. I undertook to be the guide, but
night coming on before we could reach the place, we
lost our way. Sometimes we were in swamps, up to the
middle in water; and when we reached dry land, we
could not tell whether we were walking toward the
ship, or wandering farther away. Every step increased
our uncertainty. The night grew darker, and we were
entangled in inextricable woods, where, perhaps, the
foot of man had never trod before. That part of the
country is entirely abandoned to wild beasts, with which
it prodigiously abounds.

We were in a terrible state, having neither light, food,
nor arms, and expecting a tiger to rush from behind
every tree. The stars were clouded, and we had no
compass to form a judgment which way we were going.
Had things continued thus, we had probably perished;
but it pleased God no beast came near us. After some
hours' perplexity, the moon arose, and pointed out the
eastern quarter. It appeared then, as we had expected,
that, instead of drawing nearer to the seaside, we had

been penetrating into the country. By the guidance of the moon, we at length came to the waterside, a considerable distance from the ship. We got safe on board without any other inconvenience than what we suffered from fear and fatigue.

These and many other deliverances were all at that time entirely lost upon me. The admonitions of conscience, which from successive repulses had grown weaker and weaker, at length entirely ceased. For a space of many months, if not for some years, I cannot recollect that I had a single check of that sort. At times I have been visited with sickness, and have believed myself near to death, but I had not the least concern about the consequences. I seemed to have every mark of final impenitence and rejection; neither judgments nor mercies made the least impression on me.

SAILS FOR HOME

Our business being finished, we left Cape Lopez, and after a few days' stay at the island of Annabona, to lay in provisions, we sailed homeward, about the beginning of January, 1748. From Annabona to England, without touching at any intermediate port, is a very long navigation, perhaps more than seven thousand miles, if we include the circuit necessary to be made on account of the trade winds.

We sailed first westward, till near the coast of Brazil, then northward, to the banks of Newfoundland, with the usual variations of wind and weather, and without meeting anything extraordinary. On these banks we stopped half a day to fish for cod. This was then chiefly for diversion; we had provisions enough, and little expected those fish to be all we should have to subsist on.

We left the banks March 1, with a hard westerly wind which pushed us fast homeward. Because of the length of this voyage in a hot climate, the vessel was greatly out of repair, and unfit for stormy weather. The sails and cordage were worn; and many circumstances concurred to render what followed more dangerous.

On March 9, the day before our catastrophe. I carelessly took up Stanhope's Thomas á Kempis as I had often done before, to pass away the time. I read it with indifference as if it was entirely a romance. However, while I was reading this time an involuntary suggestion arose in my mind: What if these things should be true? I could not bear the force of the inference as it related to myself, therefore shut the book presently. My conscience witnessed against me once more, and I concluded that, true or false, I must abide the consequences of my own choice. I put an abrupt end to these reflections by joining in with some vain conversation that came in the way.

THE LORD'S TIME

But now *the Lord's time was come*, and the conviction I was so unwilling to receive was deeply impressed upon me. I went to bed that night in my usual security and indifference but was awakened from a sound sleep by the force of a violent sea, which broke on us. Much of it came down below and filled the cabin where I lay with water. This alarm was followed by a cry from the deck that the ship was going down or sinking. As soon as I could recover myself, I started to go up on deck, but was met on the ladder by the captain, who desired me to bring a knife with me.

While I returned for the knife, another person went

up in my place, who was instantly washed overboard. We had no leisure to lament him, nor did we expect to survive him long, for we soon found the ship was filling very fast. The sea had torn away the upper timbers on one side, and made the ship a mere wreck in a few minutes. I shall not describe the disaster in the marine dialect, which would be understood by few; therefore I can give you but a very inadequate idea of it.

Taking in all circumstances, it was astonishing, and almost miraculous, that any of us survived. We had immediate recourse to the pumps, but the water increased against all our efforts. Some of us were set to bailing in another part of the vessel, that is, to lade it out with buckets and pails. We had but eleven or twelve people for this service. Notwithstanding all we could do, she was full, or very near it. With a common cargo she would have sunk, of course, but we had a great quantity of beeswax and wood on board, which were specifically lighter than the water. As it pleased God that we received this shock in the very crisis of the gale, toward morning we were enabled to employ some means for our safety, which succeeded beyond hope.

In about an hour's time the day began to break, and the wind abated. We used most of our clothes and bedding to stop the leaks, though the weather was exceedingly cold, especially to us who had so lately left a hot climate. Over these we nailed pieces of boards, and at last perceived the water abate. At the beginning of this I was little affected. I pumped hard, and endeavored to animate myself and my companions. I told one of them that in a few days this distress would serve us to talk of over a glass of wine, but he, being a less hardened sinner than myself, replied with tears, "No, it is too late now." About nine o'clock, being almost spent with cold and labor, I went to speak with the captain, who was busy elsewhere. As I was returning, I said, almost without any meaning, "If this will not do, the Lord have mercy on us!" This (though spoken with little reflection) was the first desire I had breathed for mercy for many years. I was instantly struck with my own words. As Jehu said once, "What hast thou to do with peace?" so it directly occurred, What mercy can there be for me? I was obliged to return to the pump, and there I continued till noon. Almost every passing wave broke over my head, but we made ourselves fast with ropes, that we might not be washed away. Indeed, I expected that every time the vessel descended into the sea, she would rise no more. I dreaded death now, and my heart foreboded the worst, if the Scriptures, which I had long since opposed, were true. Still I was but half convinced, and remained for a space of time in a sullen frame, a mixture of despair and impatience. I thought that if the Christian religion were true, I could not be forgiven, and was therefore expecting, and almost at times wishing, to know the worst.

LETTER VIII

VOYAGE HOMEWARD

MARCH 21 is a day to be remembered by me. I have never suffered it to pass wholly unnoticed since the year 1748. On that day the Lord sent from on high and delivered me out of deep waters. I continued at the pump from three in the morning till near noon, and then I could do no more I went and lay down upon my bed, uncertain, and almost indifferent, whether I should rise again. In an hour's time I was called. Not being able to pump, I went to the helm, and steered the ship till midnight, expecting a short interval for refreshment.

I had here leisure and opportunity to think of my former religious professions, the calls, warnings, and deliverances I had met with, the licentious course of my life, particularly my unparalleled effrontery in making the gospel the subject of profane ridicule. I thought, allowing the Scripture premises, there never was, nor could be, such a sinner as myself. Then, comparing the advantages I had broken through, concluded at first that my sins were too great to be forgiven.

The Scriptures seemed to say the same. I had formerly been well acquainted with the Bible, and many passages upon this occasion returned to my memory,

particularly those awful passages, Proverbs 1:24-31, He-
brews 6:4-6 and II Peter 2:20, which seemed so exactly
to suit my case and character as to bring with them a
presumptive proof of a divine original. Thus, as I have
said, I waited with fear and impatience to receive my
inevitable doom.

Yet, though I had thoughts of this kind, they were
exceedingly faint and disproportionate. It was not till
long after, perhaps several years, when I had gained
some clearer views of the infinite righteousness and
grace of Jesus Christ my Lord, that I had a deep and
strong apprehension of my state by nature and practice.
Perhaps till then I could not have borne the sight. So
wonderfully does the Lord proportion the discoveries of
sin and grace. He knows our frame, and that if He were
to put forth the greatness of His power, a poor sinner
would be instantly overwhelmed and crushed like a
moth.

THE EXERCISES OF HIS MIND

When I saw beyond all probability there was still
hope of respite, and heard about six in the evening that
the ship was freed from water, there arose a gleam of
hope. I thought I saw the hand of God displayed in our
favor and I began to pray. I could not utter the prayer
of faith; I could not draw near to a reconciled God and
call Him Father. My prayer was like the cry of ravens,
which yet the Lord does not disdain to hear. I now
began to think of that Jesus whom I had so often derid-
ed. I recollected the particulars of His life and of His
death—a death for sins not His own, but for those who
in their distress should put their trust in Him. And now
I chiefly wanted evidence. The comfortless principles of

"I went to the helm, and steered the ship till midnight."

infidelity were deeply riveted, and I rather wished than believed that these things were real facts.

The great question now was how to obtain faith. I speak not of an appropriating faith, of which I then knew neither the nature nor necessity; but how I should gain assurance that the Scriptures were of divine inspiration, and a sufficient warrant for the exercise of trust and hope in God. One of the first helps I received, in consequence of a determination to examine the New Testament more carefully, was from Luke 11:13. I had been sensible that to profess faith in Jesus Christ, when in reality I did not believe His history, was no better than a mockery of the heart-searching God; but here I found a Spirit spoken of, which was to be communicated to those who ask it. I reasoned thus: If this book is true, the promise in this passage is true likewise. I have need of that very Spirit by which the whole was written, in order to understand it. He has promised here to give that Spirit to those who ask, I must therefore pray, and if it is of God, He will make good His own word. My purposes were strengthened by John 7:17. I concluded that though I could not say from my heart that I believed the gospel, yet I would for the present take it for granted, and that by studying it in this light I should be more and more confirmed in it.

If what I am writing could be perused by our modern infidels, they would say (for I know their manner) that I was very desirous to persuade myself into this opinion. I confess I was; and so would they be, if the Lord should show them, as He was pleased to show me at that time, the absolute necessity of some expedient to interpose between a righteous God and a sinful soul. In the gospel I saw at least a peradventure of hope, but on every other side I was surrounded with black, unfathomable despair.

The wind was now moderate, but continued fair, and we were drawing nearer to our port. We began to recover from our consternation, though we were greatly alarmed by our circumstances. The water having floated all our movables in the hold, all the casks of provisions had been beaten to pieces by the violent motion of the ship. Our live stock, such as pigs, sheep and poultry, had been washed overboard in the storm.

All the provisions we saved, except the fish I mentioned, and some food intended for the hogs (and there was but little of this left), would have subsisted us but a week at scanty allowance. The sails, too, were mostly blown away so that we advanced but slowly even while the wind was fair. We imagined ourselves about a hundred leagues from the land, but were in reality much farther. Thus we proceeded with an alternating between hope and fear. My leisure time was chiefly employed in reading and meditating on the Scriptures, and praying to the Lord for mercy and instruction.

DISAPPOINTMENTS

Things continued thus for four or five days, or perhaps longer. We were awakened one morning by the joyful shouts of the watch upon deck proclaiming the sight of land. The dawning was uncommonly beautiful. The light, just strong enough to discover distant objects, presented us with a gladdening prospect. It seemed a mountainous coast, about twenty miles from us, terminating in a cape or point. A little farther, two or three small islands, or hummocks, seemed to be rising out of the water. The appearance and position seemed exactly answerable to our hopes, resembling the northwest extremity of Ireland, which we were steering for. We congratulated each other, having no doubt that if the wind continued, we should be in safety and plenty the next day.

The remainder of our brandy (a little more than a pint) was, by the captain's orders, distributed among us. We likewise ate up the residue of our bread for joy at this welcome sight, and were in the condition of men suddenly reprieved from death. While we were thus alert, the mate, with a graver tone than the rest, sunk our spirits by saying that he hoped it might prove land at last. If one of the common sailors had first said this the rest would have beat him for raising such an unreasonable doubt. It brought on, however, warm debates and disputes whether it was land or not. The case was soon unanswerably decided. The day was advancing fast, and in a little time one of our fancied islands began to grow red from the approach of the sun which soon arose just under it. We had been prodigal too hastily; our land was nothing but clouds. In half an hour more the whole appearance was dissipated.

Seamen have often known deceptions of this sort, but in our extremity we were very loath to be undeceived. However, we comforted ourselves, that though we could not see the land yet, we should soon, if wind continued fair. But alas! we were deprived of this hope also. That very day our fair wind subsided and the next morning the gale sprung up from the southwest, directly against us, and continued for more than a fortnight. The ship was so wrecked that we were obliged to keep the kind always on the broken side, unless the weather was quite moderate. With the wind in that quarter we were driven still farther from our port to the northward of all Ireland, as far as the Lewis, or western islands of Scotland, but a long way to the west. In a word, our station deprived us of any hope of being relieved by other vessels. It may, indeed, be questioned, whether our ship was not the very first to be in that part of the ocean at that season of the year.

Provisions now began to grow very short. Half of a salted cod was a day's subsistence for twelve people. We had plenty of fresh water, but not a drop of liquor, no bread, hardly any clothes, and very cold weather. We had incessant labor with the pumps, to keep the ship above water. Much labor and little food wasted us fast, and one man died. Yet our sufferings were light in comparison with our fears. We had a terrible prospect of being either starved to death or reduced to feed upon one another. Our expectations grew darker every day; and I had a further trouble peculiar to myself.

The captain, whose temper was quite soured by distress, was hourly reproaching me as the sole cause of the calamity. He was confident that if I was thrown overboard, and not otherwise, they should be preserved from death. He did not intend to make the experiment, but the continual repetition of this in my ears gave me much uneasiness, especially as my conscience seconded his words. I thought it very probable that all that had befallen us was on my account. I was at last found out by the powerful hand of God.

However, as we proceeded I began to conceive hopes greater than all my fears. When we were ready to give up all for lost, and despair was on every countenance, the wind came about to the very point we wished it, so as best to suit that broken part of the ship which must be kept out of the water. As gently as our few remaining sails could bear it continued (though at an unsettled time of the year) till we once more were called up to see the land. We saw the island Tory, and the next day anchored in Lough Swilly, Ireland. This was April 8, just four weeks after the damage we sustained from the sea. When we came into this port, our very last victuals were boiling in the pot. Before we had been there two hours, the wind began to blow with great violence. If we had continued at sea that night in our shattered, enfeebled condition, we would to all human appearance, have gone to the bottom. *About this time I began to know that there is a God who hears and answers prayer.* How many times has He appeared for me since this great deliverance! Yet, alas! how distrustful and ungrateful is my heart unto this hour!

LETTER IX

RELIGIOUS AWAKENINGS

BEFORE I PROCEED, I would look back a little, to give you some further account of the state of my mind. The straits of hunger, cold, weariness, and the fears of sinking and starving, I shared in common with others. But besides these I felt a heart-bitterness which was properly my own. No one else on board was impressed with any sense of the hand of God in our danger and deliverance.

No temporal dispensations can reach the heart unless the Lord Himself applies them. My companions in danger were either quite unaffected, or soon forgot, but it was not so with me. I was not any wiser or better than they, but the Lord was pleased to vouchsafe me peculiar mercy. I was the most unlikely person in the ship to receive an impression, having been often before quite stupid and hardened in the very face of great dangers, and having always before hardened my neck more and more after every reproof. I can see no reason why the Lord singled me out for mercy but this, "that so it seemed good to Him"; and to show by one astonishing instance that "with Him nothing is impossible."

BECOMES MORE SERIOUS AND EARNEST

There were no persons on board to whom I could speak with freedom concerning the state of my soul, none from whom I could ask advice. As to books, I had a New Testament, Stanhope, already mentioned, and a volume of Bishop Beveridge's Sermons, one of which, upon our Lord's Passion, affected me much. In perusing the New Testament, I was struck with several passages: the fig tree (Luke 13); the case of St. Paul (I Timothy 1); but particularly the prodigal (Luke 15). I thought the prodigal had never been so exemplified as by myself. The goodness of the father in receiving, nay, in running to meet such a son, as an illustration of the Lord's goodness to returning sinners, gained upon me.

I continued much in prayer; the Lord had interposed so far to save me, and I hoped He would do more. Outward circumstances helped to make me still more serious and earnest in crying to Him who alone could relieve me. Sometimes I thought I could be content to die even for want of food, if I might but die a believer. Thus far I was answered, that before we arrived in Ireland I had satisfactory evidence in my own mind of the truth of the gospel and its exact suitableness to all my needs. I saw that God might declare not only His mercy but also His justice in the pardon of sins on account of the obedience and sufferings of Jesus Christ. By that time I embraced the sublime doctrine of "God manifest in the flesh, reconciling the world to Himself."

I had no idea of those systems which allow the Saviour no higher honor than that of an upper servant, or at the most a demigod. I stood in need of an Almighty Saviour, and such an one I found described in the New Testament. The Lord had wrought a marvelous thing: I was no longer an infidel. I heartily renounced my former profaneness; was seriously disposed, and sincerely touched with a sense of undeserved mercy in being brought safe through so many dangers; I was sorry for my past misspent life and purposed an immediate reformation; I was freed from the habit of swearing which seemed to have been deeply rooted in me as a second nature. To all appearance, I was a new man.

DEPENDING CHIEFLY UPON HIS OWN RESOLUTIONS

I cannot doubt that this change, so far as it prevailed, was wrought by the Spirit and power of God, yet I was greatly deficient in many respects. In some degree, I sensed my more enormous sins, but I was little aware of the innate evils of my heart. I had no apprehension of the spirituality and extent of the law of God. The hidden life of a Christian, that of communion with God by Jesus Christ, and dependence on Him for hourly supplies of wisdom, strength, and comfort, was a mystery of which I had as yet no knowledge. I acknowledged the Lord's mercy in pardoning what was past, but depended chiefly upon my own resolution to do better for the time to come.

I had no Christian friend of faithful minister to advise me that my strength was no more than my righteousness. I began to inquire for serious books, but not having spiritual discernment, I frequently made a wrong choice. I was not brought in the way of evangelical preaching or conversation, except a few times when I heard but understood not, until six years later. Those things the Lord was pleased to show me gradually. I learned them here a little, and there a little, by painful experience, apart from ordinary means, and in the same evil company and bad examples I had known for some time. From this period I could no more make a mock of sin, or jest with holy things; I no more questioned the truth of Scripture, or quenched the rebukes of conscience. I consider this as the beginning of my return to God, or rather of His return to me, but I cannot consider myself to have been a believer in the full sense of the word till a considerable time afterward.

I have told you that in the time of our distress we had fresh water in abundance. This was a considerable relief to us, especially as our diet was mostly salt fish without bread. We drank plentifully, and were not afraid of wanting water; yet our stock was much nearer the end than we expected. We supposed that we had six large butts of water on board. It was well that we were safe in Ireland before we discovered that five of them were empty, having been moved out of their places by the violent agitation when the ship was full of water. If we had found this out while we were at sea, it would have greatly heightened our distress, as we would have drunk more sparingly.

IN IRELAND: A SERIOUS PROFESSOR

While the ship was refitting at Lough Swilly, I repaired to Londonderry. I lodged at an exceedingly good house, where I was treated with much kindness, and soon recovered my health and strength. Twice a day I went to the prayers at church, and determined to receive the sacrament the next opportunity. At length the day came. I rose very early, was very particular and earnest in my private devotion, and, with the greatest solemnity, engaged myself to be the Lord's forever, and only His. This was not a formal, but a sincere surrender, under a warm sense of mercies recently received. For want of a better knowledge of myself, and the subtlety of Satan's temptations, I was later seduced to forget these vows. However, though my views of the gospel salvation were very indistinct, I experienced a peace and satisfaction in the ordinance that day to which I had been hitherto a perfect stranger.

The next day I went shooting with the mayor of the city, and some other gentlemen. As I climbed up a steep bank, pulling my shotgun after me, in a perpendicular direction, it went off so near my face as to burn away the corner of my hat. Thus when we think ourselves in the greatest safety, we are no less exposed to danger than when all seems conspiring to destroy us. The divine providence which is sufficient to deliver us in our utmost extremity is equally necessary in the most peaceful situation.

During our stay in Ireland, I wrote home. The vessel I was in had not been heard of for eighteen months, and had been given up for lost long before. My father had no more expectation of hearing that I was alive; but he received my letter a few days before he left London. He was just going as governor of York Fort, in Hudson's Bay, and he never returned. He sailed before I landed in England. He had purposed to take me with him, but God designing otherwise, one hindrance or another delayed us in Ireland until it was too late. I received two or three affectionate letters from him, but I never had the pleasure of seeing him again. I had hopes that, in three years more, I should have had an opportunity of asking forgiveness for the uneasiness my disobedience had caused him, but the ship that was to have brought him home came without him.

Before his departure, my father paid visit to my friends in Kent, and gave his consent to the union which had been so long talked of. Thus, when I returned, I found I had only the consent of one person to obtain; with her I stood at as great an uncertainty as the first day I saw her.

RESTORATION IN SOME MEASURE

I arrived at Liverpool the latter end of May, 1748, about the same day that my father sailed from the Nore; but the Lord had found me another father in the gentleman whose ship had brought me home. He received me with great tenderness, and the strongest expressions of friendship and assistance, which he has since made good. To him, as the instrument of God's goodness, I owe my all. Yet it would not have been in the power even of this friend to have saved me effectually, if the Lord had not met with me on my way home. Till then I was like the man possessed of the legion. No arguments, no persuasion, no views of interest, no remembrance of the past or regard to the future, could have constrained me within the bounds of common prudence. But now I was, in some measure, restored to my senses.

My friend immediately offered me the command of a ship, but upon mature consideration, I declined for the present. Hitherto unsettled and careless, I thought I had better make another voyage first, learn to obey, and acquire further insight and experience in business before I ventured to undertake such a charge.

The mate of the vessel I came home in was given the

command of a new ship, and I engaged to go as mate to him. I made a short visit to London, but had only one opportunity of seeing the one I loved. I always was exceedingly awkward in pleading my own cause in our conversation. But after my return to Liverpool, I put the question in such a manner by letter, that she could not avoid, unless I had greatly mistaken her, coming to some sort of decision. Her answer, though cautious, satisfied me. I collected from it, that she was free from any other engagement, and not unwilling to wait the event of the voyage I had undertaken.

LETTER X

ADVENTURES AS A SLAVE DEALER

IMAGINE A NUMBER OF VESSELS, at different times and from different places, bound to the same port. There are some things in which all would agree—the compass steered by, the port in view, the general rules of navigation, would be the same for all. In other respects they would differ. Perhaps no two of them would meet with the same distribution of winds and weather. Some we see set out with a favorable wind; but when they almost think their passage secured, they are checked by adverse blasts. After enduring much hardship and danger, and frequent expectations of shipwreck, they barely escape and reach the desired haven.

Others meet the greatest difficulties at first. They put forth in a storm, and are often beaten back; at length their voyage proves favorable, and they enter the port with a rich and abundant entrance. Some are hard beset with cruisers and enemies, and obliged to fight their way through. Others meet with little remarkable in their passage.

THE EXPERIENCES OF BELIEVERS

Is it not thus in the spiritual life? All true believers walk by the same rule, and mind the same things: the

Word of God is their compass; Jesus is both their polar
star and their sun of righteousness; their hearts and
their faces are all set Zion-ward. They are as one body,
animated by one spirit; yet their experience, formed
upon these common principles, is far from being uniform. The Lord in His first call, and His following
dispensations, regards the situation, temper and talents
of each, and the particular services or trials He has
appointed them for. All are exercised at times, yet some
pass through the voyage of life much more smoothly
than others. But He "Who walketh upon the wings of
the wind, and measures the water in the hollow of His
hand," will not suffer any in His charge to perish in the
storms, though for a season, perhaps, many of them are
ready to give up hope.

We must not, therefore, make the experience of others, in all respects, a rule to ourselves, nor our own a
rule to others. These are common mistakes, and pro-
ductive of many more. My case has been extraordinary;.
I have hardly met a single one resembling it. Few, very
few, have been recovered from such a dreadful state.
The few that have been thus favored have generally
passed through the most severe convictions, and after
the Lord has given them peace, their future lives have
been usually more zealous, bright, and exemplary than
common.

On the one hand, my convictions were very moderate, and far below what might have been expected. On
the other hand, my first beginnings in a religious course
were as faint as can be imagined. I never knew that
season alluded to (Jer. 2:2; Rev. 2:4) usually called the
time of the first love. Who would not expect to hear,
that after such a wonderful, unhoped for deliverance as

I had received, and after my eyes were in some measure enlightened to see things aright, I should immediately cleave to the Lord and His ways with purpose of heart, and consult no more with flesh and blood?

Alas! It was far otherwise with me. I had learned to pray, I set some value upon the Word of God and was no longer a libertine, but my soul still cleaved to the dust. Soon after my departure from Liverpool I began to grow slack in waiting upon the Lord. I grew vain and trifling in my conversation. Though my heart smote me often, my armor was gone, and I declined fast. By the time I arrived at Guinea, I seemed to have forgotten all the Lord's mercies. Profaneness excepted, I was almost as bad as before. The enemy prepared a train of temptations, and I became his easy prey. For about a month, he lulled me asleep in a course of evil, of which a few months before, I could not have supposed myself any longer capable.

THE DECEITFULNESS OF SIN

"Take heed, lest any of you be hardened through the deceitfulness of sin!" Sin first deceives, and then it hardens. I was now fast bound in chains; I had little desire, and no power at all to free myself. I would at times reflect how it was with me, but if I attempted to struggle, it was in vain. I was just like Samson, when he said, "I will go forth, and shake myself, as at other times"; but the Lord was departed, and he felt himself helpless in the hands of his enemies. By the remembrance of this interval, the Lord has often reminded me what a poor creature I am in myself, incapable of standing a single hour without continual fresh supplies of strength and grace from the fountain-head.

At length the Lord, whose mercies are infinite, interposed on my behalf. My business in this voyage, while upon the coast, was to sail from place to place in the longboat to purchase slaves. The ship was at Sierra Leone, and I then at the Plantanes, the scene of my former captivity. I was in easy circumstances, courted by those who formerly despised me. The lime-trees I had planted were growing tall, and promised fruit the following year, at which time I had expectations of returning with a ship of my own.

VISITED WITH A VIOLENT FEVER

But none of these things affected me, till the Lord again interposed to save me. He visited me with a violent fever, which broke the fatal chain, and once more brought me to myself. But oh, what a prospect! My past dangers and deliverances, my earnest prayers in the time of trouble, my solemn vows before the Lord at His table, and my ungrateful returns for all His goodness were all brought to my mind at once I began to wish that the Lord had suffered me to sink into the ocean when I first besought His mercy. For a little while I concluded the door of hope to be shut; but this continued not long. Weak and almost delirious, I arose from my bed and crept to a secluded part of the island; there I found a renewed liberty to pray. I made no more resolves, but cast myself before the Lord to do with me as He should please. I do not remember that any particular text, or remarkable discovery was presented to my mind; but, in general, I was enabled to hope and believe in a crucified Saviour.

The burden was removed from my conscience, and not only my peace but my health was restored, I cannot say instantaneously, but I recovered from that hour. When I returned to the ship, two days afterward, I was perfectly well before I got on board. From that time, I trust I have been delivered from the power and dominion of sin: though, as to the effects and conflicts of sin dwelling in me, I still "groan, being burdened." I now began again to wait upon the Lord. Though I have often grieved His Spirit and foolishly wandered from Him since (when, alas! shall I be more wise?), His powerful grace has preserved me from such black declensions as this I have last recorded. I humbly trust in His mercy and promises, that He will be my guide and guard to the end.

My leisure hours in this voyage were chiefly employed in learning the Latin language which I had now entirely forgot. This desire took place from an intimation I had seen in one of Horace's odes in a magazine. By dint of hard industry, often waking when I might have slept, I made some progress before I returned, and not only understood the sense and meaning of many odes, and some of the epistles, but began to relish the beauties of the composition, and acquired a spice of what Mr. Law calls classical enthusiasm. Indeed, I had Horace more in my mind than some who are masters of the Latin tongue, for my helps were so few that I generally had the passage fixed in my memory before I could fully understand its meaning.

During the eight months we were upon the coast, I was exposed to innumerable dangers and perils from burning suns and chilling dews, winds, rains, and thunder-storms, in the open boat; on shore, from long journeys through the woods, and the temper of the natives, who are in many places cruel, treacherous, and watching opportunities for mischief. Several boats in that time were cut off and several white men poisoned. In my own boat I buried six or seven people with fevers. When going on shore or returning in the little canoes, I have been more than once or twice overturned by the violence of the surf or breach of the sea, and brought to land half dead, for I could not swim. An account of the escapes I still remember would swell to several pages; many more I have perhaps forgotten. I shall select only one instance as a specimen of that wonderful providence which watched over me for good.

A PROVIDENTIAL ESCAPE

When our trade was finished, and we were near sailing to the West Indies, the only remaining service I had to perform in the boat was to assist in bringing the wood and water from the shore. We were then at Rio Cestors. I used to go into the river in the afternoon with the sea-breeze, procure my cargo in the evening, and return on board in the morning with the land-wind. Several of these little voyages I had made; but the boat was old, and almost unfit for use.

One day, having dined on board, I was preparing to return to the river, as formerly, I had taken leave of the captain, received his orders, was ready in the boat, and just going to let go our ropes, and sail from the ship. In that instant the captain came up from the cabin, and called me on board again. I went, expecting further orders, but he said, that I should remain that day in the ship, and ordered another man to go in my place. I was surprised at this, as the boat had never been sent away without me before, and asked him the reason; he could give me no reason but that so he would have it.

Accordingly the boat went without me, and never returned. She sank that night in the river, and the person who had taken my place was drowned. I was much struck when we received news of the event the next morning. The captain himself, a stranger to religion, could not help being affected. He declared that he had no other reason for countermanding me at that time, but that it came suddenly into his mind to detain me.

LETTER XI

MARRIAGE—A COMMANDER OF A SHIP

A FEW DAYS after I was thus wonderfully saved from an unforseen danger, we sailed for Antigua, and from thence proceeded to Charlestown in South Carolina. In this place there are many serious people, but I knew not where to find them. Indeed I was not aware of a difference, but supposed that all who attended public worship were good Christians. I was as much in the dark about preaching, not doubting that whatever came from the pulpit must be very good. I had two or three opportunities of hearing a dissenting minister, named Smith, who, by what I have known since, I believe to have been an excellent and powerful preacher of the Gospel. There was something in his manner that struck me, but I did not rightly understand him. The best words that men can speak are ineffectual till explained and applied by the Spirit of God. He alone can open the heart. It pleased the Lord, for some time, that I should learn no more than what He enabled me to collect from my own experience and reflection.

My conduct was now very inconsistent. Almost every day, when business would permit, I used to retire into the woods and fields and I trust I began to taste the sweets of communion with God in the exercises of prayer and praise. Yet I frequently spent the evenings in vain and worthless company. My relish for worldly diversions was much weakened, and I was more a spectator than a sharer in their pleasures, but I did not as yet see the necessity of separation. As my compliance with custom and company was chiefly due to want of light, rather than to an obstinate attachment, the Lord was pleased to preserve me from what I *knew* was sinful. I had for the most part peace of conscience, and my strongest desires were toward the things of God.

Not understanding the force of that precept, "Abstain from all appearance of evil," I very often ventured upon the brink of temptation; yet the Lord was gracious to my weakness, and did not suffer the enemy to prevail against me. I was gradually led to see the inconvenience and folly of one thing after another, and when I saw it the Lord strengthened me to give it up. But it was some years before I was delivered from occasional compliance in many things which at this time I do not allow myself.

We finished our voyage, and arrived in Liverpool. When the ship's affairs were settled, I went to London, and from thence, as you may suppose, to Kent. More than seven years had elapsed since my first visit. Through the overruling goodness of God, while I seemed abandoned to myself, and blindly following my own headstrong passions, I was guided to the accomplishment of my wishes. Every obstacle was now removed. I had renounced my former follies, and my interest was established. Friends on all sides consenting, the point was now entirely between ourselves. Accordingly our hands were joined on February 1, 1750.

The satisfaction I have found in this union has been greatly heightened by reflection on the former disagreeable contrasts I had passed through, and the singular mercy and providence of the Lord in bringing it to pass. If you look back to the beginning of my sixth letter, you will allow, that few persons have known more either of the misery or happiness of which human life is capable. How easily, at a time of life when I was so little capable of judging (but a few months more than seventeen), might my affections have been fixed where they could have met with no return, or the heaviest disappointment! The long delay was a mercy. Had I succeeded a year or two sooner, before the Lord was pleased to change my heart, we would have been mutually unhappy, even as to the present life. "Surely mercy and goodness have followed me all my days."

RESTING IN THE GIFT AND FORGETTING
THE GIVER

But, alas! I soon began to feel that my heart was still hard, and ungrateful to the God of my life. This crowning mercy, which raised me to all I could ask or wish in a temporal view, and which ought to have resulted in obedience and praise, had a contrary effect. I rested in the gift, and forgot the Giver. My poor narrow heart was satisfied. A cold and careless frame, as to spiritual things, took place, and gained ground daily. Happily for me, in June I received orders to repair to Liverpool. This roused me from my dream. I need not tell you that I found the pains of absence and separation as great as my preceding pleasure. It was hard very hard to part, especially as conscience suggested how little I deserved that we should be spared to meet again.

But the Lord supported me. I was a poor, faint, idolatrous creature, but I had now some acquaintance with the way of access to the throne of grace by the blood of Jesus, and peace was soon restored. Yet through all the following voyage, my irregular and excessive affections were as thorns in my eyes, and often made my other blessings tasteless and insipid. But He who doth all things well overruled this likewise for good. It became an occasion of quickening me in prayer both for my wife and myself; it increased my indifference for company and amusement; and it habituated me to a kind of voluntary self-denial, which I later learned to improve to a better purpose.

While I remained in England, we corresponded every post. While I was at sea, I constantly kept up the practice of writing two or three times a week, if weather and business permitted, though no conveyance homeward offered for six or eight months together. As not one of my letters miscarried, I have nearly 200 pages now lying in my bureau (dresser) of that correspondence.

This relief, by which I contrived to soften the intervals of absence, had a good effect beyond my first intention. It caused me to think and write upon a great variety of subjects, and I acquired a greater readiness of expressing myself than I should otherwise have attained. As I gained more ground in religious knowledge, my letters became more serious. At times, I still find an advantage in looking them over, especially as they remind me of many providential incidents, and the state of my mind at different periods in these voyages, which would otherwise have escaped my memory.

I sailed from Liverpool in August, 1750, commander of a good ship. Having now the command and care of thirty persons, I endeavored to treat them with humanity, and set them a good example. I established public worship, according to the liturgy, twice every Lord's day, officiating myself. Farther than this I did not proceed while I continued in that employment.

Having now much leisure, I prosecuted the study of the Latin with good success. In the space of two or three voyages I became tolerably acquainted with the best classics. I read Terence, Virgil, and several pieces of Cicero, and the modern classics, Buchanan, Erasmus, and Cassimir. I conceived a design of becoming a Ciceronian myself, and thought it would be a fine thing indeed to write pure and elegant Latin. I wrote some essays, but by this time the Lord was pleased to draw me nearer to Himself, and to give me a fuller view of the "Pearl of great price," the inestimable treasure hid in the field of the Holy Scriptures. For the sake of this, I was willing to part with all my newly-acquired riches.

I began to think that life was too short, especially my life, for such elaborate trifling. Neither poet nor historian could tell me a word of Jesus, and I therefore applied myself to those who could. The classics were at first confined to one morning in the week, and at length quite laid aside. I prefer Buchanan's Psalms* to a whole shelf of Elzevirs. I have gained so much of the Latin as enables me to read any useful or curious book that is published in that language. More than this I do not care about. About the same time, and for the same reason, I laid aside the mathematics. I found that they not only cost me much time, but engrossed my thoughts too far; my head was literally full of schemes. I was weary of cold contemplative truths which can neither warm nor

*George Buchanan, Scottish historian and scholar, 1506-82.

amend the heart, but rather tend to aggrandize self. I found no traces of this wisdom in the life of Jesus, or the writings of Paul. I do not regret that I have had some opportunities of knowing the first principles of these things, but I praise the Lord that He inclined me to stop in time. While I was "spending my labor for that which is not bread," He was pleased to set before me "wine and milk, without money and without price."

My first voyage was fourteen months, through various scenes of danger and difficulty, but nothing very remarkable. As I intend to be more particular with regard to the second voyage, I shall only say that I was preserved from every harm. Having seen many fall on my right hand and on my left, I was brought home in peace, and restored to where my thoughts had often been directed. That was November 2, 1751.

LETTER XII

SEAFARING LIFE

IN THE INTERVAL between my first and second voyage after my marriage, I began to keep a sort of diary, a practice which I have since found of great use. I had in this interval repeated proofs of the ingratitude and evil of my heart. A life of ease in the midst of my friends, and the full satisfaction of my wishes, was not favorable to the progress of grace. Yet, upon the whole, I gained ground. I became acquainted with books which gave me a further view of Christian doctrine and experience: particularly Scougall's "Life of God in the Soul of Man," Hervey's "Meditations," and the "Life of Colonel Gardiner." I heard none but the common sort of preaching, neither had I the advantage of Christian acquaintance. I was likewise greatly hindered by a cowardly, reserved spirit, for I was afraid of being thought precise. Though I could not live without prayer, I did not propose it even to my wife, till she herself urged it. I was far from those expressions of zeal and love which seem so suitable to the case of one who has had much forgiven. When the returning season called me abroad again, I sailed from Liverpool, in a new ship, July, 1752.

A seafaring life is necessarily excluded from the benefit of public ordinances and Christian communion. In other respects, I know not any calling that affords greater advantages to an awakened soul, for promoting the life of God in the soul; especially to a person who has the command of a ship. He has it in his power to restrain gross irregularities in others, and to dispose of his own time. It is more so in African voyages, as these ships carry a double portion of men and officers to most others. This made my department very easy; and excepting the occasional hurry of trade on the coast, afforded me leisure.

DIVINE PROVIDENCE AND COMMUNION

In these circumstances, one is out of the reach of innumerable temptations, with opportunity and turn of mind disposed to observe the wonders of God in the great deep. The two noblest objects of sight, the expanded heavens and the expanded ocean, are continually in view. Interpositions of divine providence, in answer to prayer, occur almost every day. All these are helps to quicken and confirm the life of faith, and, in a good measure, supply to a religious sailor the want of those advantages which can be enjoyed only upon the shore. Indeed, though my knowledge of spiritual things was at this time very small, I sometimes look back with regret upon these scenes. I never knew sweeter or more frequent hours of divine communion than in my two last voyages to Guinea, when almost secluded from society on shipboard, or when on shore amongst the natives.

I have wandered through the woods, reflecting on the singular goodness of the Lord to me, in a place where, perhaps, there was not a person that knew Him for some thousand miles around me. Many a time, upon these occasions, I have restored the beautiful lines of Propertius to their right owner: lines full of blasphemy and madness when addressed to a creature, but full of comfort and propriety in the mouth of a believer:

Sic ego desertis possim bene vivere sylvis,
Quo nulla humano sit via treta pide:
Tu mihi curarum requies, in nocte vel atra
Lumen, et in solis tu mihi turba locis.

PARAPHRASED
In desert wood, with Thee, my God,
Where human footsteps never trod,
        How happy could I be!
Thou my repose from care, my Light
Amidst the darkness of the night,
        In solitude my company.

SLAVE TRADING

In the course of this voyage I was wonderfully preserved in the midst of many obvious and unforeseen dangers. At one time there was a conspiracy among my own people to turn pirates, and take the ship from me. When the plot was nearly ripe, and they waited only a convenient opportunity, two of them concerned in it were taken ill one day. One of them died, and he was the only person I buried while on board. This suspended the affair, and led to its discovery, or the consequences might have been fatal. The slaves on board were likewise frequently plotting insurrections. Sometimes they were upon the very brink of mischief, but it was always disclosed in due time. When I have thought myself most secure, I have been suddenly alarmed with danger; and when I have almost despaired of life, a sudden deliverance has been vouchsafed me.

"The slaves on board were likewise frequently plotting insurrections."

IN DEATHS OFTEN

At one time I was at a place called Mana, near Cape Mount, where I had transacted very large concerns. At the time I had some debts and accounts to settle, which required my attendance on shore, and I intended to go the next morning. I left the ship, according to my purpose, but when I came near the shore, the surf ran so high that I was almost afraid to attempt landing. I had often ventured at a worse time, but I felt an inward hindrance and backwardness which I could not account for. The surf furnished a pretext, and after hesitating for about half an hour, I returned to the ship without doing my business, which I never did but that morning in all the time I used that trade. I soon perceived the reason for all this. The day before I intended to land, a scandalous and groundless charge had been laid against me, by whose instigation I could never learn, which greatly threatened my honor and interest, both in Africa and England, and would perhaps, humanly speaking, have affected my life, if I had landed according to my intention. I was very uneasy for a few hours, but was soon comforted. I heard no more of my accusation till the next voyage, when it was publicly acknowledged to be a malicious calumny, without the least shadow of a ground.

Such were the vicissitudes and difficulties through which the Lord preserved me. Faith and patience were sharply exercised, but suitable strength was given. As such things did not occur every day, the study of the Latin was renewed and carried on from time to time when business would permit. I was mostly very regular in the management of my time. I allotted eight hours for sleep and meals, eight hours for exercise and devotion, and eight hours to my books. Thus, by diversifying my engagements, the whole day was agreeably filled up; and I seldom found a day too long, or an hour to spare. My studies kept me employed; otherwise they were hardly worth the time they cost, as they led me to an admiration of false models and false maxims, an almost unavoidable consequence of an admiration of classic authors. Abating what I have attained of the language, I think I might have read Cassandra or Cleopatra to as good purpose as I read Livy, whom I now account an equal romancer, though in a different way.

From the coast I went to St. Christopher's; and here my idolatrous heart was its own punishment. The letters I expected from Mrs. Newton were by mistake forwarded to Antigua, which had been at first proposed as our port. As I was certain of her punctuality in writing, if alive, I concluded, by not hearing from her, that she was surely dead. This fear affected me more and more. I lost my appetite and rest; I felt an incessant pain in my stomach; and in about three weeks' time I was under the weight of an imaginary stroke. I felt some severe symptoms of that mixture of pride and madness which is commonly called a broken heart. Indeed I wonder that this case is not more common than it appears to be. How often do the potsherds of the earth presume to contend with their Maker! and what a wonder of mercy is it that they are not all broken! However, my complaint was not all grief; conscience had a share. I thought my unfaithfulness to God had deprived me of her, especially my backwardness in speaking of spiritual things, which I could hardly attempt even to her.

It was the thought that I had lost invaluable, irrecoverable opportunities, which both duty and affection should have engaged me to improve, that chiefly stung me. I thought I would have given the world to know that she was living, that I might at least discharge my engagements by writing, though I was never to see her again. This was a sharp lesson, but I hope it did some good. When I had thus suffered some weeks, I thought of sending a small vessel to Antigua. I did so, and it brought me several packets. These restored my health and peace, and gave me a strong contrast of the Lord's goodness to me, and my unbelief and ingratitude toward Him.

August, 1753, I returned to Liverpool. My stay was very short at home that voyage, only six weeks. In that time nothing very memorable occurred. I shall therefore continue with an account of my third and last voyage.

LETTER XIII

RELINQUISHES A SEAFARING LIFE

BEFORE I SAILED on my third voyage, I met with a young man who had formerly been a midshipman, my intimate companion on board the *Harwich*. He was, at the time I first knew him, a sober youth; but I had found too much success in my unhappy attempts to infect him with libertine principles. When we met at Liverpool, our acquaintance was renewed upon the ground of our former intimacy. He had good sense, and had read many good books. Our conversation frequently turned upon religion, and I was very desirous to repair the mischief I had done him. I gave him a plain account of the manner and reason of my change, and used every argument to persuade him to relinquish his infidel schemes. When I sometimes pressed him so close that he had no other reply to make, he would remind me that I was the first person who had given him an idea of his liberty. This occasioned me many mournful reflections.

He was then going master to Guinea himself; but before his ship was ready, his merchant became a bankrupt, which cancelled his voyage. As he had no more expectations for that year, I offered to take him with me as a companion, that he might gain a knowledge of the coast. The gentleman who employed me promised to provide for him upon his return. My view in this was not so much to serve him in his business, as to have an opportunity of debating the point with him at leisure. I hoped, in the course of my voyage, my arguments, example, and prayers might have some good effect on him. My intention in this step was better than my judgment, and I had frequent reason to repent it. He was exceedingly profane, and grew worse and worse. I saw in him a lively picture of what I had once been; it was very inconvenient to have it always before my eyes.

Besides, he was not only deaf to my remonstrances himself, but labored all he could to counteract my influence upon others. His spirit and passions were exceedingly high; it required all my prudence and authority to hold him in any degree of restraint. He was a sharp thorn in my side for some time. At length I had an opportunity on the coast of buying a small vessel which I supplied with a cargo from my own. I gave him the command, and sent him away to trade on the ship's account.

When we parted I repeated and enforced my best advice. I believe his friendship and regard were as great as could be expected, when our principles were so diametrically opposite. He seemed greatly affected when I left him, but my words had no weight. When he found himself at liberty from under my eye, he indulged every appetite. His violent irregularities, added to the heat of the climate, threw him into a malignant fever, which carried him off in a few days. He died convinced, but not changed. The account I had from those who were with him was dreadful. His rage and despair struck them all with horror. He pronounced his own fatal doom before he expired, without any appearance that he either hoped or asked for mercy. I thought this awful contrast might not be improper to give you, as a stronger view of the distinguishing goodness of God to me, the chief of sinners.

I left the coast in about four months, and sailed for St. Christopher's. Hitherto I had enjoyed a perfect state of health, equally in every climate for several years, but on this passage I was visited with a fever, which gave me a very near prospect of eternity. I have obtained liberty to enclose you three or four letters, which will more clearly illustrate the state and measure of my experience at different times than anything I can say at present. One of them was written at this period, when I could hardly hold a pen and had some reason to believe I should write no more. I had not that "full assurance," which is so desirable at a time when flesh and heart fail. But my hopes were greater than my fears, and I felt a silent composure of spirit which enabled me to await the event without much anxiety.

"ABLE TO SAVE TO THE UTTERMOST"

My trust, though weak in degree, was fixed upon the blood and righteousness of Jesus. The words, "He is able to save to the uttermost," gave me great relief. I was for a while troubled with a very singular thought; whether it was a temptation, or that the fever disordered my faculties, I cannot say. I seemed not so much afraid of wrath and punishment, as of being lost and overlooked amid the myriads continually entering the unseen world. What is my soul, thought I, among such an innumerable multitude? Perhaps the Lord will take no notice of me. I was perplexed thus for some time;

but at last a text of Scripture occurred to my mind, and put an end to the doubt: "The Lord knoweth them that are His." In about ten days, beyond the hopes of those about me, I began to mend; and by the time of our arrival in the West Indies I was perfectly recovered.

A CHRISTIAN CAPTAIN

For about the space of six years, the Lord was pleased to lead me in a secret way. I had learned something of the evil of my heart; I had read the Bible over and over with several good books, and had a general view of gospel truths; but my conceptions were in many respects, confused, not having in all this time met with one acquaintance who could answer my inquiries.

Upon my arrival at St. Christopher's this voyage, I found a captain of a ship from London, whose conversation was greatly helpful to me. He was a man of experience in the things of God, and of a lively communicative turn. We discovered each other by some casual expressions in mixed company, and soon became, so far as business would permit, inseparable. For nearly a month we spent every evening together on board each other's ship alternately, and often prolonged our visits till toward daybreak. I was all ear; he not only increased my understanding, but his teaching warmed my heart. He encouraged me to open my mouth in social prayer; he taught me the advantage of Christian conversation; he put me upon an attempt to make my profession more public, and to venture to speak for God.

From him, rather from the Lord by him, I received an increase of knowledge; my conceptions became clearer and more evangelical; and I was delivered from a fear which had long troubled me—the fear of relapsing into my former apostasy. Now I began to understand the security of the covenant of grace, and to expect to be preserved, not by my own power and holiness, but by the mighty power and promise of God, through faith in an unchangeable Saviour. He likewise gave me a general view of the errors and controversies of the times, things to which I had been entirely a stranger, and finally directed me where to apply in London for further instruction. With these newly-acquired advantages, I left him, and my passage home gave me leisure to digest what I had received. I had much comfort and freedom during those seven weeks, and my sun was seldom clouded. I arrived in Liverpool, August, 1754.

HIS VIEW OF THE SLAVE TRADE

By the beginning of November I was again ready for the sea, but the Lord saw fit to overrule my plans. During the time I was engaged in the slave trade, I never had the least scruple as to its lawfulness. I was upon the whole satisfied with it as the appointment providence had marked out for me. It was, indeed, accounted a genteel employment, usually very profitable, though to me it did not prove so, the Lord seeing that a large increase of wealth would not be good for me. However, I considered myself as a sort of jailer and I was sometimes shocked with an employment that was perpetually connected with chains, bolts, and shackles. In this view I had often prayed that the Lord in His own time would be pleased to place me in a more humane calling, and where I might have more frequent fellowship with His people and ordinances. I longed to be freed from these long separations from home, which very often were hard to bear. My prayers were answered, though in a way I little expected.

I was within two days of sailing, and to all appearance in good health as usual. In the afternoon as I was sitting with Mrs. Newton, drinking tea, and talking over past events, I was taken by a seizure which deprived me of sense and motion, and left me no sign of life but that of breathing. It lasted about an hour. When I recovered, a pain and dizziness in my head induced the physicians to judge it would not be safe or prudent for me to proceed on the voyage. By the advice of my friend to whom the ship belonged, I resigned the command the day before she sailed. Thus I was unexpectedly called from that service, and freed from the consequences of that voyage. The person who went in my place, most of the officers, and many of the crew died, and the vessel was brought home with great difficulty.

MRS. NEWTON'S ILLNESS

Now disengaged from business, I left Liverpool, and spent most of the following year at London and in Kent. But I entered upon a new trial. You will easily conceive that Mrs. Newton was not an unconcerned spectator, when I was taken ill. The blow that struck me reached her in the same instant, but she did not feel it until her apprehensions on my account began to subside. As I grew better, she was thrown into a disorder, which no physician could define, or medicines remove. Without any of the ordinary symptoms of a consumption, she decayed almost visibly. She became so weak that she could hardly bear anyone to walk across the room she was in. I was placed for about eleven months in what Dr. Young calls the *dreadful post of observation, darker every hour.*

After my settlement at Liverpool, the Lord was pleased to restore Mrs. Newton by His own hand, when all hopes from ordinary means were at an end. But before this took place, I have some other particulars to mention.

LETTER XIV

THE STUDENT OF SCRIPTURE

BY THE DIRECTIONS I had received from my friend at St. Kitts, I soon found religious acquaintances in London. I usually attended upon Mr. Brewer's ministry when in town. From him I received much help, both in public and private, for he was pleased to favor me with his friendship. His kindness, and the intimacy between us continued and increased, and of all my many friends I am most deeply indebted to him. The late Mr. H— was my second acquaintance, a man of choice spirit, and abundant zeal for the Lord's service. I enjoyed his correspondence till near the time of his death. Upon Mr. Whitefield's return from America, my two good friends introduced me to him. Although I had little personal acquaintance with him until afterward, his ministry was exceedingly helpful to me. I had likewise access to some religious societies, and became known to many excellent Christians in private life. Thus, when at London, I lived at the fountainhead for spiritual advantages. When I was in Kent, it was very different. Though I found some serious persons there, the fine, variegated woodland country afforded me advantages of another kind. At least some hours every day, I passed in retirement, when the weather was fair, sometimes in the thickest woods, sometimes on the highest hills, where almost every step varied the prospect. It has been my custom for many years to perform my devotional exercises *sub die*, when I have opportunity. These rural scenes have some tendency both to refresh and to compose my spirits. A beautiful, diversified prospect gladdens my heart. When I am withdrawn from the noise and petty works of men, I consider myself as in the great temple which the Lord has built for His own honor.

THE LORD'S COMFORTABLE PRESENCE

The country between Rochdale and Maidstone, bordering upon the Medway, was well suited to the turn of my mind. Were I to go over it now, I could point to many a place where I have either earnestly sought, or happily found, the Lord's comfortable presence with my soul. I lived sometimes at London, and sometimes in the country, till the autumn of the following year. All this while I had two trials more or less upon my mind. The first and principal was Mrs. Newton's illness. She grew worse, and I had daily more reason to fear that the hour of separation was at hand. When faith was exercised, I was in some measure resigned to the Lord's will; but too often my heart rebelled, and I found it hard either to trust or to submit.

I had likewise some concern about my future. The African trade was overdone that year, and my friends did not care to fit out another ship till mine returned. I was in some suspense, but a provision of food and raiment has seldom been a cause of great solicitude to me. I found it easier to trust the Lord in this case than in the former, but this was first answered.

TIDE SURVEYOR AT LIVERPOOL

In August I received word that I was nominated to the office of tide surveyor. These places are usually obtained, or at least sought, by reason of much interest and application; but this came to me unsought and unexpected. I knew my good friends in Liverpool had endeavored to procure another post for me, but found it taken. I found afterward that the place I had missed would have been very unsuitable for me. This, which I had no thought of, was the very thing I could have wished for. It afforded me much leisure, and the liberty of living in my own way. The good hand of the Lord was in this event.

But when I gained this point, my distress in the other was doubled. I was obliged to leave Mrs. Newton in the greatest extremity of pain and illness. The physicians could do no more, and I had no ground of hope that I should see her again alive, but this—nothing is impossible with the Lord. I had a severe conflict, but faith prevailed. I found the promise remarkably fulfilled, of strength proportioned to my need. The day before I set out, and not till then, the burden was entirely taken from my mind. I was strengthened to resign both her and myself to the Lord's disposal, and departed from her in a cheerful frame. Soon after I was gone, she began to mend. She recovered so fast, that in about two months I had the pleasure to meet her at Stone, on her journey to Liverpool.

Since October, 1755, we have been comfortably settled at Liverpool, and all my circumstances have been as remarkably smooth and uniform. My trials have been light and few, but I still find, in the experience of every day, the necessity of a life of faith.

HIS PRINCIPAL TRIAL

My principal trial is the body of sin and death, which makes me often sigh out the apostle's complaint, "O wretched man . . . !" With him likewise I can say, "I thank God through Jesus Christ our Lord." I live in a barren land, where the knowledge of and power of the Gospel is very low, yet here are a few of the Lord's people. This has been a useful school to me, where I have studied more leisurely the truths I gathered up in London.

I brought with me a considerable stock of notional truth, but have found that there is no effectual teacher but God. We can receive no more than He is pleased to communicate; no knowledge is truly useful but what is made by experience. Many things I thought I had learned would not stand in an hour of temptation, until I had in this way learned them over again. Since the year 1757, I have had an increasing acquaintance in the West Riding of Yorkshire, where the Gospel flourishes greatly. This has been a good school to me; I have conversed at large among all parties, without joining any. In any attempts to hit the golden mean, I have sometimes been drawn too near the different extremes, yet the Lord has enabled me to profit by my mistakes. I am still a learner, and the Lord still condescends to teach me. I have attained but very little, but I trust in Him to carry on His work in my soul, and by His grace and providence to increase my knowledge of Him, and of myself.

DIVORCED FROM THE CLASSICS

When I was settled in a house, and found my business would afford me much leisure, I considered in what manner I should improve it. Determined "to know nothing but Jesus Christ and Him crucified," I resolved to pursue nothing but in subservience to this main purpose. This resolution divorced me, as I have already hinted, from the classics and mathematics. My first attempt was to learn enough Greek to enable me to understand the New Testament and Septuagint. When I had made some progress this way, I entered upon the Hebrew the following year. Two years afterward, having seen some advantages from the Syriac version, I began with that language.

I have not attained, or ever aimed at, a critical skill in any of these. I had no business with them, but as in reference to something else. I only wanted the signification of scriptural words and phrases; and for this I availed myself of others who sustained the drudgery before me. In the Hebrew, I can read the historical books and psalms with tolerable ease, but in the prophetical parts, I am frequently obliged to have recourse to lexicons. However, I am able, with such helps as are at hand, to judge for myself the meaning of any passage I have occasion to consult. Beyond this I do not think of proceeding, if I can find better employment, for I would rather be useful to others, than die with the reputation of an eminent linguist.

Together with these studies I have kept up a course of reading of the best writers in divinity that have come to my hand, in the Latin and English tongues, and some French, which I picked up at times while I used the sea. But in these two or three years I have given myself chiefly to writing, and have not found time to read many books besides the Scriptures.

In all my literary attempts, I have been obliged to strike out my own path, by the light I could acquire from books, as I have not had a teacher or assistant since I was ten years of age.

HIS DESIRE TO SERVE THE LORD

I have told you that it was my dear mother's hope that I enter the ministry. Her death, and the life in which I afterward engaged, seemed to cut off the probability. The first desires of this sort in my own mind arose from a reflection on Galatians 1:23, 24: "But they had heard only, that he which persecuted us in times past now preached the faith which once he destroyed. And they glorified God in me." I could wish for such a public opportunity to testify the riches of divine grace. I thought I was, above most living, a fit person to proclaim that faithful saying, that "Jesus Christ came into the world to save the chief of sinners." As my life had been full of remarkable turns, and I seemed selected to show what the Lord could do, I had some hope that perhaps sooner or later He might call me into his service.

It was this hope that determined me to study the original Scriptures, but it remained an imperfect desire in my own breast, till it was recommended to me by some Christian friends. I questioned the thought when first seriously proposed to me, but afterward set apart some weeks to consider the case, to consult my friends, and to entreat the Lord's direction. The judgment of my friends, and many things that occurred, tended to convince me.

My first thought was to join the Dissenters, but preferring the Established Church in some respects, I solicited ordination from the late Archbishop of York. I need not tell you I met a refusal. At present (1763), my desire to serve the Lord is not weakened, but I am not so hasty to push myself forward as I was formerly. It is sufficient that He knows how to dispose of me, and that He both can and will do what is best. To Him I command myself. I trust that His will and my true interest are inseparable. To His Name be glory.

FURTHER ACCOUNT

OF JOHN NEWTON'S LIFE, ABRIDGED FROM
THE WORK OF THE REV. R. CECIL

JOHN NEWTON, having expressed near the end of his narrative the motives which induced him to aim at a regular appointment to the ministry in the Church of England, mentions the refusal he met with in first making the attempt. On Dec 16, 1758, Mr. Newton applied to the Archbishop of York for ordination. The Bishop of Chester, having countersigned his testimonials, directed him to Dr. Newton, the archbishop's chaplain. He was referred to the secretary, who informed him that he had "represented the matter to the archbishop, but his Grace was inflexible in supporting the rules and canons of the Church."

Newton had made some small attempts at Liverpool, in a way of preaching or expounding. Many wished him to engage more at large in ministerial employments. He was so inclined, and he expresses his motives in a letter to his wife: "The death of the late Rev. Mr. Jones of St. Saviour's has pressed this concern more closely upon my mind. I fear it must be wrong, after having so solemnly devoted myself to the Lord for His service, to wear away my time, and bury my talents in silence, because I have been refused orders in the Established Church after all the great things He has done for me. . . .

The exercises of my mind upon this point, I believe, have not been peculiar to myself. I have known several persons, sensible, pious, of competent abilities, and cordially attached to the Established Church, who, being wearied out with repeated refusals of ordination, and perhaps, not having the advantage of such an adviser as I had, have at length struck into the itinerant path, or settled among the Dissenters. Some of these, yet living, are men of respectable characters, and useful in their ministry."

APPOINTED TO THE PARISH OF OLNEY

In the year 1764, Newton had the curacy of Olney proposed to him, and was recommended by Lord Dartmouth to Dr. Green, Bishop of Lincoln. He was ordained. In the parish of Olney he found many who had not only had evangelical views of the truth, but had also long walked in the light and experience of it. The vicarage was in the gift of the Earl of Dartmouth, the nobleman to whom he addressed the first twenty-six letters in his *Cardiphonia*. The earl was a man of real piety, and most amiable disposition; he formerly appointed the Rev. Moses Brown vicar of Olney. Mr. Brown was an evangelical minister, and a good man; he had afforded wholesome instruction to the parishioners of Olney, and had been the instrument of a sound conversion in many of them.

Newton continued at Olney nearly sixteen years prior to his removal to St. Mary Woolnoth, to which he was afterward presented by John Thornton.

Providence seems to have appointed Newton's residence at Olney, among other reasons, for the relief of the depressed mind of the poet Cowper.

Of great importance also was the vicinity of his residence to the Rev. Thomas Scott, then curate of Ravenstone and Weston Underwood, a man whose ministry and writings have since been so useful to mankind.

THE PATIENCE OF A CHRISTIAN UNDER PAIN

In the year 1776, Newton was afflicted with a tumor which had formed on his thigh. On account of it growing more large and troublesome, he resolved to undergo the experiment of extirpation. This obliged him to go to London for the operation, which was successfully performed. The trial did not seem to have affected him as a painful operation, so much as a critical opportunity in which he might fail in demonstrating the patience of a Christian under pain. "I felt," said he, "that being enabled to bear a very sharp operation, with tolerable calmness and confidence, was a greater favor granted to me than the deliverance from my malady."

While he thus continued faithfully discharging his duties of watching for the temporal and eternal welfare of his flock, a dreadful fire broke out at Olney, October, 1777. Mr. Newton took an active part in comforting and relieving the sufferers. He collected money for them.

If a minister, like the subject of these Memoirs, be alive to the interest of his own soul, and that of the souls committed to his charge, or as the apostle expresses it, "to save himself, and those that hear him," he may depend upon meeting in his own experience the truth of that declaration, "Yea, all that will live godly in Christ Jesus shall suffer persecution," in one form of it or another.

I have heard him say on such an occasion, "When God is about to perform any great work, He generally permits some great opposition to it. Suppose Pharaoh

"Newton was ordained and served the parish of Olney."

had acquiesced in the departure of the children of Israel, or that they had met with no difficulties in the way. They would, indeed, have passed from Egypt into Canaan with ease, but they, as well as the Church in all future ages, would have been great losers. The wonder-working God would not have been in those extremities, which make His arm so visible. A smooth passage here would have made but a poor story."

But under such disorders, he in no one instance that I have ever heard of was tempted to depart from the precept and example of his Master. He continued to bless them that persecuted him, "knowing that the servant of the Lord must not strive, but be gentle unto all men, apt to teach, patient." To the last day he spent among them he went straight forward, "in meakness instructing those that opposed, if God peradventure might give them repentance to the acknowledging of the truth."

HIS LITERARY WORK

Before we take leave of Olney, the reader must be informed of another part of his labors. He had published a volume of Sermons dated Liverpool, January 1, 1760. In 1762, he published his *Omicron*, to which his letters, signed Vigil, were afterward annexed. In 1764 appeared his *Narrative*. In 1767 a volume of Sermons, preached at Olney. In 1769, his *Review of Ecclesiastical History*; and in 1770 a volume of hymns, of which some were composed by Mr. Cowper, and distinguished by a C. prefixed to them. To these succeeded, in 1781, his valuable work *Cardiphonia*.

AT ST. MARY WOOLNOTH

From Olney, Newton was removed to the rectory of

the united parishes of St. Mary Woolnoth and St. Mary Woolchurch Haw, Lombard Street, on the presentation of his friend, Mr. Thornton.

Some difficulty arose concerning Mr. Thornton's right of presentation, the latter being claimed by a nobleman; the question was, therefore, at length brought before the House of Lords, and determined in favor of Mr. Thornton. He preached his first sermon in these parishes, December 19, 1779, from Ephesians 4:15, "speaking the truth in love." It contained an affectionate address to his parishioners, and was directly published for their use.

Placed in the center of London, in an opulent neighborhood, he had now a course of service to pursue, in several respects different from his former at Olney. Being, however, well acquainted with the Word of God, and the heart of man, he proposed no new weapons of warfare for pulling down the strongholds of sin and Satan around him.

THE IMPORTANCE OF HIS NEW SPHERE

I have heard him speak with great feeling of his last important station. "That one," said he, "of the most ignorant, the most miserable, and the most abandoned of slaves should be plucked from his forlorn state of exile on the coast of Africa, and at length be appointed minister of the parish of the first magistrate of the first city in the world; that he should there not only testify of such grace, but stand up as a singular instance and monument of it; that he should be enabled to record it in his history, preaching, and writings to the world at large, is a fact I can contemplate with admiration, but never sufficiently estimate." This reflection, indeed, was so present to his mind that he seldom passed a single day anywhere, but that he was found referring to the strange event in one way or other.

Being of the most friendly and communicative disposition, his house was open to Christians of all ranks and denominations. Here, like a father among his children he used to entertain, encourage and instruct his friends, especially younger ministers, or candidates for the ministry. Here also the poor, the afflicted, and the tempted found an asylum and a sympathy which they could scarcely find, in an equal degree, anywhere else.

HIS TIMELY HINTS AND SAVINGS

His timely hints were often given with much point and profit to the numerous acquaintances who surrounded him in his public station. Some time after he had published his *Omicron*, and described the three stages of growth in religion, from the blade, the ear, and the full corn in the ear, distinguishing them by the letters A, B, and C, a conceited young minister wrote to him, telling him that he read his own character accurately drawn in that of C. Newton wrote in reply, that in drawing the character of C, or full maturity, he had forgotten to add, until now, one prominent feature of C's character, namely, that C never knew his own face.

"It grieves me," said he, on another occasion, "to see so few of my wealthy parishioners come to church. I always consider the rich as under greater obligation to the preaching of the gospel than the poor. For at church, the rich must hear the whole truth as well as others. There they have no escape. But let them once get home, you will be troubled to get at them. When you are admitted, you are so fettered with punctilio, so interrupted and damped with the frivolous conversation of their friends, that, as Archbishop Leighton says, 'it is well if your visit does not prove a blank or a blot.' "

He used to improve every occurrence which he could, with propriety, bring into the pulpit. One night he found a notice put up at St. Mary Woolnoth's upon which he commented a great deal when he came to preach. The notice was to this effect: "A young man, having come to the possession of a very considerable fortune, desires the prayers of the congregation, that he may be preserved from the snares to which it exposes him." "Now if the man," said Newton, "had lost a fortune, the world would not have wondered to have seen him put up a notice, but this man has been better taught."

Coming out of his church on a Wednesday, a lady stopped him on the steps, and said, "The ticket, of which I held a quarter, has drawn a prize of ten thousand pounds. I know you will congratulate me upon this occasion." "Madam," said he, "as for a friend under temptation, I will endeavor to pray for you."

I could not help observing, one day, how much he was grieved with the mistake of a minister, who appeared to pay too much attention to politics. "For my part," said he, "I have no temptation to turn politician, and much less to inflame a party in these times. When a ship is leaky, and a mutinous spirit divides the company on board, a wise man would say, 'My good friends, while we are debating, the water is gaining on us; we had better leave the debate, and go to the pumps.' I endeavor," continued he, "to turn my people's eyes from instruments to God. I am continually attempting to show them how far they are from knowing either the matter of fact, or the matter of right. I inculcate our great privileges in this country, and advise a discontented man to take a lodging for a little while in Russia or Prussia."

I remember to have heard him say, when speaking of his continual interruptions, "I see in this world two heaps of human happiness and misery; now if I can take but the smallest bit from one heap, and add to the other, I carry a point. If, as I go home, a child has dropped a penny, and if, by giving it another, I can wipe away tears, I feel I have done something. I should be glad indeed to do greater things, but I will not neglect this. When I hear a knock at my study door, I hear a message from God; it may be a lesson of instruction, perhaps a lesson of patience; but since it is His message, it must be interesting."

But it was not merely under his own roof that his benevolent aims were thus exerted. He was found ready to take an active part in relieving the miserable, directing the anxious, or recovering the wanderer, in whatever state or place he discovered such.

THE HAND OF GOD IN EVERY EVENT

Newton used to spend a month or two annually at the house of some friend in the country. He always took an affectionate leave of his congregation before he departed, and spoke of his return as uncertain, considering the variety of incidents which might prevent it. Nothing was more remarkable than his constant habit of regarding the hand of God in every event, however trivial it might appear to others. On every occasion, in the concerns of every hour, in matters public or private, like Enoch, he "walked with God."

Newton experienced a severe shock soon after he came to St. Mary's, and while he resided on Charles Square, in the death of his niece, Miss Eliza Cunningham. He loved her with the affection of a parent, and she was, indeed, truly lovely. With the most amiable natural qualities, she possessed real piety. Mr. and Mrs. Newton saw her gradually sink into death. Fully prepared to meet her heavenly Father, she departed October 6, 1785, aged fourteen years and eight months.

But "clouds return after the rain"—a greater loss than that of Miss Cunningham was to follow. These Memoirs show the more than ordinary affection Newton felt for her who had been so long his idol, as he used to call her. I shall add but one more instance, out of many that might easily be collected.

Being with him at the house of a lady at Blackheath, we stood at a window which had a view of Shooter's Hill. "Ah," said he, "I remember the many journeys I took from London to stand at the top of that hill, in order to look toward the part in which Mrs. Newton then lived. I could not see the spot itself after traveling several miles, for she lived far beyond what I could see from the hill. But it gratified me even to look toward the spot, and this I did always once and sometimes twice a week." "Why," said I, "this is more like one of the vagaries of romance than of real life." "True," he replied, "but real life has extravagances that would not be permitted to appear in a well-written romance."

In such an excessive attachment, it is evident how keenly he must have felt it as he observed the progress of her illness. This will be manifest from the following account, It was added to his publication, *"Letters to a Wife"*:

SOME PARTICULARS RESPECTING THE CAUSE,
PROGRESS AND CLOSE OF THE LAST ILLNESS OF MY
LATE DEAR WIFE

My dear wife had naturally a good constitution and was favored with good spirits to the last. But she sustained a violent shock in the year 1754, when I was suddenly attacked by a seizure (I know not of what kind) which left me for about an hour no sign of life but breathing. This made a sudden change in her, and subjected her from that time to a variety of chronic complaints. I believe she spent ten years out of the forty that she was spared to me (if all the days of her sufferings were added together) in illness. But she had likewise long intervals of health.

Before our removal from Liverpool, she received a blow upon her left breast. This occasioned her some pain and anxiety for a little time, but soon wore off. A small lump remained, but I heard no more of it for many years. Her tenderness for me made her conceal it as long as possible. I have often since wondered at her success, and how I could be kept so long ignorant.

In October, 1788, she applied, unknown to me, to a friend of mine, an eminent surgeon. Her plan was, if he approved it, to submit to an operation, to arrange with him, that it might be performed in my absence, and before I could know of it. But the surgeon told her that the malady was too far advanced. The tumor, the size of half a melon, was too large to be removed without danger of her life. He could give her little advice, but to keep herself as quiet, and her mind as easy as possible. The pains to which she was exposed were generally rendered tolerable by the use of laudanum;

to which, however, she had a dislike, little short of an antipathy.

I cannot easily describe the composure and resignation with which she gave me this recital the day after her interview with the surgeon, nor the sensations of my mind while I heard it. My conscience told me that I well deserved to be wounded where I was most sensitive; that it was my duty to submit with silence to the will of the Lord. But I strongly felt that, unless He was pleased to give me this submission, I was more likely to toss like a wild bull in a net, in defiance of my better judgment.

Soon after, the Lord was pleased to visit our dear adopted daughter with a dreadful fever. She (Miss Catlett) was brought very near to the grave indeed; we once or twice thought her dead. But He, who in judgment remembers mercy, restored her and still preserves her, to be the chief temporal comfort of my old age.

This heavy trial lasted during the whole of a very severe winter. This by no means promoted that tranquility of mind which my good friend wished my dear wife to preserve. She was often much fatigued, and much alarmed. Next to each other, this dear child had the nearest place both in her heart and mine. The effects were soon apparent: as the spring of 1789 advanced, her malady rapidly increased. Her pains were almost incessant, and often intense, and she could seldom lie one hour in bed in the same position. Oh! my heart, what didst thou suffer!

But in April God mercifully afforded relief, and gave such a blessing to the means employed that her pains ceased. Though I believe she never had an hour of perfect ease, she felt little of the distressing pains incident to her malady, from that time to the end of her life.

In the close of the summer she was able to go to Southampton. She returned tolerably well, and was twice at church the first week after she came home. She then went no more out, except in a coach for a little air and exercise, but she was cheerful, tolerably easy, slept as well as most people who are in perfect health, and could receive and converse with her kind friends who visited her.

Under this trying discipline I learned more than ever to pity those whose sufferings are aggravated by poverty. Our distress was not small, yet we had everything within reach that could in any degree refresh or relieve. We had faithful and affectionate servants who were always willingly engaged, even beyond their power, in attending and assisting her by night and by day. What must be the feelings of those who, when afflicted with grievous diseases, pine away, unpitied, unnoticed, without help, and, in a great measure, destitute of common necessaries? This reflection, among others, contributed to quiet my mind, and to convince me that I had much more cause for thankfulness than for complaint.

For about a year her spirits were good, her patience was exemplary. There was a cheerfulness in her looks and her language that was wonderful. Often the liveliness of her remarks has forced a smile upon us, when the tears were in our eyes. Whatever little contrivances she formed for her amusement in the course of the day, she would attend to nothing till she had finished her stated reading of the Scripture, to which she gave much time and attention. I have her Bible in which almost every principal text, from the beginning to the end, is marked in the margin with a pencil, by her own dear hand. The good Word of God was her medicine and her food, while she was able to read it. She read Dr. Watts's Psalms and Hymns, and the Olney Hymns, in the same manner. There are few of them in which one, two, or more verses are not thus marked. In many, which I suppose she read more frequently, every verse is marked.

One addition to our trial remained. It had been her custom, when she went from her sofa to her bed, to exert herself for my encouragement, to show me how well she could walk. But it pleased the Lord that, by some alteration, which affected her spine, she was disabled from moving herself; and other circumstances rendered it extremely difficult to move her. It has taken five of us nearly two hours to move her from one side of the bed to the other. At times, even this was impracticable, so that she had lain more than a week exactly in the same spot. All this was necessary on my account. The rod had a voice, and it was the voice of the Lord. I understood the meaning no less plainly than if He had spoken audibly from heaven, and said, "Now contemplate your idol! Now see what *she* is, whom you once presumed to prefer to *Me*!" Even this bitter cup was sweetened by the patience and resignation which He gave her. When I would say, "You suffer greatly," her answer usually was, "I suffer indeed; but, not greatly." And she often expressed her thankfulness that, though her body was immovable, she was still permitted the use of her hands.

One of the last concerns she felt in this world was when my honored friend, patron, and benefactor, the late John Thornton, Esq. was removed to a better one. She revered him, I believe, more than she did any person upon earth: and she had reason. Few had nearer access, to know and admire his character, and perhaps none were under greater, if equal, obligations to him than we. She knew of his illness, but was always afraid to inquire after the event, nor should I have ventured to inform her. But the occasion requiring me to leave her for four or five hours, when I hardly expected to find her alive at my return, I was constrained to give her the reason of my absence. She eagerly replied, "Go, by all means; I would not have you stay with me upon any consideration." I put the funeral ring I was favored with into her hands; she put it first to her lips, and then to her eyes, bedewing it with her tears. She survived him more than a month.

Her head became so affected that I could do little more than sit and look at her. Our intercourse by words was nearly broken off. She could not easily bear the sound of the gentlest foot upon the carpet, nor of the softest voice. On Sunday, December 12, when I was preparing for church in the morning, she sent for me, and we took a final farewell. She faintly uttered an endearing appellation, which was familiar to her, and gave me her hand, which I held, while I prayed by her bedside. We exchanged a few tears: but I was almost as unable to speak as she was. I returned soon after, and said, "If your mind, as I trust, is in a state of peace, it will be a comfort to me if you can signify it by holding up your hand." She held it up, and waved it to and fro several times.

That evening, her speech, her sight, and, I believe, her hearing wholly failed. She continued perfectly composed, without taking notice of anything, or showing any sign of pain or uneasiness, till Wednesday evening, toward seven o'clock. She then began to breathe very hard: her breathing might be called groaning, for it was heard in every part of the house; but she lay quite still, with a placid countenance, as if in a gentle slumber. There was no start or struggle, nor a feature ruffled. I took my post by her bedside, and watched her nearly three hours, with a candle in my hand, till I saw her breathe her last, on December 15, 1790, a little before ten in the evening.

When I was sure she was gone, I took off her ring, according to her repeated injunction, and put it upon my own finger. I then kneeled down with the servants who were in the room, and returned the Lord my unfeigned thanks for her deliverance, and her peaceful dismission.

About two or three months before her death, when I was walking up and down the room, offering disjointed prayers, from a heart torn with distress, a thought suddenly struck me, with unusual force: The promises of God must be true; surely the Lord will help me if I am willing to be helped. It occurred to me that we are often led, from a vain complacency in what we call our sensibility, to indulge that unprofitable grief, which both our duty and our peace require us to resist to the utmost of our power. I instantly said aloud, "Lord, I am helpless indeed in myself, but I hope I am willing, without reserve, that Thou shouldest help me."

It had been much upon my mind, from the beginning of this trial, that I was a minister, and that the eyes of many were upon me; that my turn of preaching had very much led me to endeavor to comfort the afflicted, by representing the gospel as an effectual remedy for every evil, a full compensation for every want or loss to those who truly receive it. Though a believer may be afflicted, he cannot be properly unhappy, unless he gives way to selfwill and unbelief. I had often told my hearers that trial, if rightly improved, was to the Christian a post of honor, affording the fairest opportunity of exemplifying the power of divine grace to the praise and glory of the Giver.

It had been my daily prayer, that I might not by impatience or despondency, be deprived of confirming, by my own practice, the doctrine which I had preached to others. I prayed that I might not give them occasion to apply to me the words of Eliphaz to Job: "Thy words have upholden him that was falling, and thou hast strengthened the feeble knees. But now it is come upon thee, and thou faintest; it touchest thee, and thou art troubled." And I had not prayed in vain. From the time that I so remarkably felt myself willing to be helped, my heart trusted in Him, and I was helped indeed. Through the whole of my painful trial I attended all my stated and occasional services, as usual. A stranger would scarcely have discovered either by words or looks, that I was in trouble. Many of our intimate friends were apprehensive that this long affliction, and especially the closing event, would overwhelm me; but it was far otherwise. It did not prevent me from preaching a single sermon, and I preached on the day of her death.

After she was gone, my willingness to be helped, and my desire that the Lord's goodness to me might be observed by others for their encouragement, made me indifferent to some laws of established custom the breach of which is often more noticed than the violation of God's commands. I was afraid of sitting at home, and indulging myself by poring over my loss. Therefore I was seen in the street, and visited some of my serious friends the very next day. I preached three times while she lay dead.

Some of my brethren kindly offered their assistance, but as the Lord was pleased to give me strength, both of body and mind, I thought it my duty to stand up in my place as formerly. After she was deposited in the vault, I preached her funeral sermon, with little more emotion than if it had been for another person. I hope that many of my hearers were comforted in their afflictions, by what they saw of the Lord's goodness to me in my time of need. It was well worth standing a while in the fire, for such an opportunity of experiencing and exhibiting the power and faithfulness of His promises.

I was not supported by lively sensible consolations, but by being enabled to recall to mind some great and leading truths of the Word of God. I saw what, indeed, I knew before, but never till then so strongly and clearly perceived that, as a sinner, I had no *right*, and as a believer, I could have no *reason* to complain. I considered her as a loan, which He who lent her to me had a right to resume whenever He pleased. As I had deserved to forfeit her every day from the first, it became me rather to be thankful that she was spared so long to me, than to resign her with reluctance when called for. His sovereignty is connected with infinite wisdom and goodness. Consequently, if it were possible for me to alter any part of His plan, I could only spoil it. Such a short-sighted creature as I, so blind to the possible consequences of my own wishes, was not only unworthy, but unable to choose well for himself; it was therefore my great mercy and privilege that the Lord condescended to choose for me. May such considerations powerfully affect the hearts of my readers under their troubles. Then I shall not regret having submitted to the view of the public that which may seem more proper for the subject of a private letter to a friend.

In the year 1790, Mr. Newton had the honorary degree of D.D. conferred upon him by the university of New Jersey, in America, and the diploma sent him. He also received a work in two volumes, dedicated to him, with the degree letters added to his name. Mr. Newton wrote the author a grateful acknowledgment for the work, but begged to decline an honor which he never intended to accept. "I am," said he, "as one born out of due time. I have neither the pretension nor wish to honors of this kind. However, therefore, the university may overrate my attainments, and thus show their respect, I must not forget myself; it would be both vain and improper were I to concur in it."

ILLNESS OF MISS E. CATLETT

Newton used to make excursions in the summer to different friends in the country, endeavoring to make these visits profitable to them and to their neighbors by his prayers and expositions of the Scriptures at their morning and evening worship. I have heard of some who were first brought to the knowledge of themselves and of God by attending his exhortations on these occasions. Indeed, besides what he undertook in a more stated way at the church, he seldom entered a room but something both profitable and entertaining fell from his lips. After the death of Miss Cunningham and Mrs. Newton, his companion in these summer excursions was his other niece, Miss Elizabeth Catlett. This young lady who had also been brought up by him and his wife with Miss Cunningham now became the object of his naturally affectionate disposition. She also became quite necessary to him by her ministrations in his latter years. She watched him, walked with him, visited wherever he went. When his sight failed, she read to him, divided his food, and was unto him all that a dutiful daughter could be.

But in the year 1801 a nervous disorder seized her, by which Newton was obliged to submit to her being separated from him. During the year it lasted, the weight of the affliction, added to his weight of years, seemed to overwhelm him.

NEWTON'S EVENTIDE

It was with a mixture of delight and surprise that the friends and hearers of this eminent servant of God beheld him bringing forth fruit in extreme age. Though almost eighty years old, his sight nearly gone, and incapable, through deafness, of joining in conversation, yet his public ministry was regularly continued, and maintained with a considerable degree of his former animation. His memory, indeed, was observed to fail, but his judgment in divine things still remained. Though some depression of spirit was observed, which he used to account for by his advanced age, his perception, taste, and zeal for the truths he had long received and taught were evident. Like Simeon, having seen the salvation of the Lord, he now only waited and prayed to depart in peace.

After Newton turned eighty, some of his friends feared he might continue his public ministry too long. They marked not only his infirmities in the pulpit, but the decrease of his strength, and his occasional depressions. On the latter, he observed that he had experienced nothing which in the least affected the principles he had felt and taught; that his depressions were the natural result of fourscore years; and that at any age, we can only enjoy that comfort from our principles which God is pleased to send. "But," I replied, "in the matter of public preaching, might it not be best to consider your work as done, and stop before you evidently discover you can speak no longer?" "I cannot stop," said he, raising his voice. "What! shall the old African blasphemer stop while he can speak?"*

In every future visit I noticed old age making rapid strides. At length his friends found some difficulty in making themselves known to him. His sight, his hearing, and his memory failed; but, being mercifully kept from pain, he generally appeared easy and cheerful. Whatever he uttered was perfectly consistent with the principles he had so long and so honorably maintained.

Newton declined in this very gradual way, till at length it was painful to ask him a question, or attempt to rouse faculties almost gone. It is quite natural to inquire, though it is not important, how such a decided character left this world. I have heard him say, when he has heard particular inquiry made about the last expressions of an eminent believer, "Tell me not how the man died, but how he lived."

NEWTON'S DEATH, DECEMBER 21, 1807

About a month before his death, Mr. Newton said, "It is a great thing to die; and when flesh and heart fail, to have God for the strength of our heart, and our

---

*Newton's last sermon was preached in October, 1806 for a fund in aid of the widows and orphans of Trafalgar.

portion for ever; I know whom I have believed, and He is able to keep that which I have committed unto Him against that day. Henceforth there is laid up for me a crown of righteousness, which the Lord, the righteous Judge, shall give me at that day."

Later to his niece, formerly Miss Catlett, he said, "I have been meditating on a subject, 'Come, and hear, all ye that fear God, and I will declare what He hath done for my soul.' "

At another time he said, "More light, more love, more liberty. Hereafter I hope, when I shut my eyes on the things of time, I shall open them in a better world. What a thing it is to live under the shadow of the wings of the Almighty! I am going the way of all flesh." And when one replied, "The Lord is gracious," he answered, "If it were not so, how could I dare to stand before Him?"

The Wednesday before he died, when asked if his mind was comfortable, he replied, "I am satisfied with the Lord's will." Newton seemed sensible to his last hour, but expressed nothing remarkable after these words. He departed December 21, 1807, and was buried in the vault of his church ten days later, having left the following injunction in a letter, for the direction of his executors:

"I propose writing an epitaph for myself, if it may be put up on a plain marble tablet near the vestry door, to the following purport:

JOHN NEWTON, CLERK,
Once an infidel and libertine,
A servant of slaves in Africa,
Was, by the rich mercy of our Lord and Saviour,
JESUS CHRIST,

Preserved, restored, pardoned,
And appointed to preach the faith
He had long laboured to destroy,
Near sixteen years at Olney, in Bucks,
And . . . years in this church.
On February 1, 1750, he married
MARY,
Daughter of the late George Catlett,
of Chatham, Kent,
He resigned her to the Lord who gave her,
On the 15th day of December, 1790.

And I earnestly desire that no other monument and no inscription but to this purport, may be attempted for me."

The following is a copy of the beginning of

MR. NEWTON'S WILL

dated June 13, 1803:

"In the name of God, Amen. I, John Newton, of Coleman Street Buildings, in the parish of St. Stephen, Coleman Street, in the city of London, clerk, being through mercy in good health and of sound and disposing mind, memory, and understanding, although in the seventy-eighth year of my age, do for the settling of my temporal concerns, and for the disposal of all the worldly estate which it hath pleased the Lord in His good providence to give me, make this my last will and testament as follows: I commit my soul to my gracious God and Saviour, who mercifully spared and preserved me, when I was an apostate, a blasphemer, and an infidel, and delivered me from that state of misery on the coast of Africa into which my obstinate wickedness had plunged me; and Who has been pleased to admit me, though most unworthy, to preach His glorious gospel. I rely with humble confidence upon the atonement, and mediation of the Lord Jesus Christ, God and Man, which I have often proposed to others, as the only foundation whereupon a sinner can build his hope, trusting that He will guard and guide me through the uncertain remainder of my life, and that He will then admit me into His presence in His heavenly kingdom. I would have my body deposited in the vault under the parish church of St. Mary Woolnoth, coffins of my late dear wife and my dear niece, Elizabeth Cunningham; and it is my desire that my funeral may be performed with as little expense as possible, consistent with decency."

SOME REMARKS

MADE BY JOHN NEWTON IN FAMILIAR CONVERSATION

When a Christian goes into the world because he sees it is his *call*, yet, while he feels it also his *cross*, it will not hurt him.

Satan will seldom come to a Christian with a gross temptation; a green log and a candle may be safely left together, but bring a few shavings, then some small sticks, and then larger, and you may soon bring the green log to ashes.

If two angels were sent from Heaven to execute a divine command, one to conduct an empire and the other to sweep a street in it, they would feel no inclination to change employments.

What some call providential openings, are often powerful temptations; the heart, in wandering, cries, Here is a way opened before me: but, perhaps, not to be trodden but rejected.

A Christian should never plead spirituality for being a sloven; if he be but a shoe cleaner, he should be the best in the parish.

My principal method of defeating heresy is by establishing truth. One proposes to fill a bushel with tares; now, if I can fill it first with wheat, I shall defy his attempts.

Many have puzzled themselves about the origin of

evil; I observe there *is* evil, and that there is a way to escape it, and with this I begin and end.

Consecrated things under the law were first sprinkled with blood, and then anointed with oil, and thenceforward were no more common. Thus under the gospel, every Christian has been a common vessel for profane purposes, but when sprinkled and anointed, he becomes separated and consecrated to God.

A spirit of adoption is the spirit of a child; he may disoblige his father, yet he is not afraid of being turned out of doors. The union is not dissolved, though the communion is. He is not well with his father, therefore must be unhappy, as their interests are inseparable.

A Christian in the world is like a man who has had a long intimacy with one, whom at length he finds out to have been the murderer of a kind father; the intimacy, after this, will surely be broken.

Candor will always allow much for inexperience. I have been thirty years forming my own views, and in the course of this time some of my hills have been sinking, and some of my valley have risen, but how unreasonable would it be to expect all this should take place in another person, and that in the course of a year or two!

Candor forbids us to estimate a character from its accidental blots. Yet it is thus that David and others have been treated.

I can conceive a living man without an arm or a leg, but not without a head or a heart; so there are some truths essential to vital religion, and which all awakened souls are taught.

A Christian is like a young nobleman who, on going to receive his estate, is at first enchanted with his prospects; this, in a course of time, may wear off, but a sense of the value of the estate grows daily.

When we first enter into the divine life, we propose to grow rich; God's plan is to make us feel poor.

Good men have need to take heed of building upon groundless impressions. Mr. Whitefield had a son, who, as he imagined, was born to be a very extraordinary man, but the son soon died, and the father was cured of his mistake.

I remember, in going to undertake the care of a congregation, I was reading, as I walked in a green lane, "Fear not, Paul, I have much people in this city." But I soon afterwards was disappointed in finding that Paul was not John, and that Corinth was not Warwick.

Christ has taken our nature into Heaven to represent us; and has left us on earth, with His nature, to represent Him.

Worldly men will be true to their principles, and if we were as true to ours, the visits between the two parties would be short and seldom.

A Christian in the world is like a man transacting his affairs in the rain. He will not suddenly leave his client because it rains; but the moment the business is done, he is off: as it is said in the Acts, "Being let go, they went to their own company."

God deals with us as we do with our children: He first speaks, then gives a gentle stroke, at last a blow.

The religion of a sinner stands on two pillars; namely, what Christ did for us in His flesh, and what He performs in us by His Spirit. Most errors arise from an attempt to separate these two.

Man is not taught anything to purpose till God becomes his teacher, and then the glare of the world is put out, and the value of the soul rises in full view. A man's present sentiments may not be accurate, but we make too much of sentiments. We pass a field with a few blades; we call it a field of wheat, but here is no wheat; no, not in perfection, but the wheat is sown, and full ears may be expected.

The word temperance in the New Testament signifies self-possession; it is a disposition suitable to one who has a race to run, and therefore will not load his pockets with lead.

Contrivers of systems on the earth are like contrivers of systems in the heavens; where the sun and moon keep the same course, in spite of the philosophers.

A man always in society is one always on the spend; on the other hand, a mere solitary is, at his best, but a candle in an empty room.

If we were upon the watch for improvement, the common news of the day would furnish it. The falling of the tower of Siloam, and the slaughter of the Galileans, were the news of the day, which our Lord improved.

Take away a toy from a child, and give him another, and he is satisfied, but if he be hungry, no toy will do. Thus as new-born babes, true believers desire the sincere milk of the Word, and the desire of grace in this way is grace.

One said that the great saints in the calendar were, many of them, poor sinners. Mrs. Newton replied, they were poor saints indeed if they did not feel that they were great sinners.

The Lord has reasons far beyond our ken for opening a wide door, while He stops the mouth of a useful preacher. John Bunyan would not have done half the good he did, if he had remained preaching in Bedford, instead of being shut up in Bedford prison.

Professors who own the doctrines of free grace, often act inconsistently with their own principles, when they are angry at the defects of others. A company of travelers fall into a pit, and one of them gets a passenger to draw him out. Now he should not be angry with the rest for falling in, nor because they are not yet out as he is; he did not pull himself out. Therefore, instead of reproaching them, he should show them pity; he should avoid, at any rate, going down upon their ground again, and show how much better and happier he is upon his own. We should take care that we do not make our profession of religion a receipt in full of all other obligations. A man truly illuminated will no more despise others, than Bartimaeus, after his own eyes were opened would take a stick and beat every blind man he met.

It is pure mercy that negatives a particular request. A miser would pray very earnestly for gold, if he believed prayer would gain it; whereas, if Christ had any favor to him He would take his gold away. A child walks in the garden in spring and sees cherries; he knows they are good fruit and therefore asks for them. "No, dear," says the father, "they are not yet ripe; stay till the season."

If I cannot take pleasure in infirmities, I can sometimes feel the profit of them. I can conceive a king to pardon a rebel, and take him into his family, and then say, "I appoint you for a season to wear a fetter. At a certain season I will send a messenger to knock it off. In the meantime this fetter will serve to remind you of your state; it may humble you and restrain you from rambling."

I have read of many wicked popes, but the worst pope I ever met with is Pope Self.

The heir of a great estate, while a child, thinks more of a few shillings in his pocket than of his inheritance. So a Christian is often more elated by some frame of heart than by his title to glory.

I feel like a man who has no money in his pocket, but is allowed to draw for all he wants upon one infinitely rich; I am, therefore, at once both a beggar and a rich man.

Sometimes I compare the troubles which we have to undergo in the course of the year to a great bundle of fagots, far too large for us to lift. But God does not require us to carry the whole at once; He mercifully unties the bundle, and gives us first one stick, which we are to carry today, and then another which we are to carry tomorrow, and so on. This we might easily manage, if we would only take the burden appointed for us each day; but we chose to increase our troubles by carrying yesterday's stick over again today, and adding tomorrow's burden to our load, before we are required to bear it.

THE NAME OF JESUS
(Song of Solomon 1:3)

How sweet the Name of Jesus sounds
   In a believer's ear!
It soothes his sorrows, heals his wounds,
   And drives away his fear.

It makes the wounded spirit whole,
   And calms the troubled breast;
'Tis manna to the hungry soul,
   And to the weary rest.

Dear Name! the Rock on which I build;
  My Shield and Hiding-place;
My never-failing Treasury fill'd
  With boundless stores of grace.

By Thee my prayers acceptance gain,
  Although with sin defiled;
Satan accuses me in vain,
  And I am own'd a child.

Jesus! my Shepherd, Husband, Friend,
  My Prophet, Priest, and King;
My Lord, my Life, my Way, my End,
  Accept the praise I bring.

Weak is the effort of my heart,
  And cold my warmest thought;
But when I see Thee as Thou art,
  I'll praise Thee as I ought.

Till then I would Thy love proclaim
  With every fleeting breath;
And may the music of Thy Name ·
  Refresh my soul in death!
                    —JOHN NEWTON